SEIDMAN AND SON

Seidman and Son

A

COMEDY IN THREE ACTS

by

Elick Moll

BASED ON HIS NOVEL

SAMUEL FRENCH, INC.

25 WEST 45th ST.   NEW YORK 36
7623 SUNSET BLVD.   HOLLYWOOD 46
LONDON - TORONTO

Seventh Avenue and 37th Street, New York, is the center of the garment industry. Here within an area of a few square blocks, more ladies' apparel is turned out —and more sedatives taken in—than in all the rest of the country combined.

The workers in the area fall into four general classes: intense, more intense, most intense and fractured.

Each day, from Brooklyn, Long Island, the Bronx, New Jersey, from buses, trains, trolleys, ferries, they converge upon the lofts. Materials pour in from all quarters of the globe. Tables are piled high with silks, cottons, woolens, acetates. Cutting machines slice through the piles like butter. Sewing machines whir. Tempers grow frayed, designing rooms echo with the clarinet wails of temperament. And all this is so that in the Elite Emporium in Chillicothe, milady may poke her head out of a wilderness of crepes and say demurely, "Isn't it infuriating. I can't find a thing to wear."

BELASCO THEATRE

Theatre Guild Productions Inc.—Joel Schenker
and Michael Kanin

PRESENT

SAM LEVENE

IN THE NEW COMEDY

SEIDMAN AND SON

BY

ELICK MOLL

BASED ON HIS NOVEL

WITH

NANCY WICKWIRE

| Frances Chaney | Hy Anzel | Martin Garner |
| Vincent Gardenia | Mitchell Jason | Stewart Moss |

AND

MORGAN STERNE

Production Designed by WILLIAM PITKIN
Associate Producer—ELLIOT MARTIN

Directed by

CARMEN CAPALBO

CAST

(In order of appearance)

MORRIS SEIDMAN........................*Sam Levene*

CONSTANCIA............................*Marian Carr*

SOPHIE SEIDMAN.....................*Frances Chaney*

JENNY SEIDMAN......................*Alberta Grant*

HAROLD SEIDMAN.....................*Stewart Moss*

MISS WEINTRAUB'S VOICE.............*Sunny Harnett*

DOREEN............................*Diana Muldaur*

JANICE.............................*Janice Carson*

LAURA MENKEN.....................*Nancy Wickwire*

LARRY KOGEN.......................*Morgan Sterne*

ROSENZWEIG............................*Hy Anzel*

MR. KARP..........................*Martin Garner*

SIDNEY............................*John Crowther*

WILENSKI.........................*Vincent Gardenia*

LEO..............................*Alfred Leberfeld*

MISS KELLEY.........................*Audrey Ward*

MR. MAGNUSON......................*Mitchell Jason*

SHELLEY...........................*Sunny Harnett*

TINA.............................*Mercedes Ospina*

EDMAE.........................*Edme Van Dyke*

HELEN SOWOLSKA.....................*Yafa Lerner*

SYNOPSIS OF SCENES

Time: The Present.

ACT ONE

SCENE 1: Dining Room of the Seidman home. 8 A.M.
SCENE 2: Seidman's Place of Business. Later that morning.

ACT TWO

SCENE 1: A Corner of Manny's Blue Room. Evening, same day.
SCENE 2: Bedroom of the Seidman home. Several hours later.
SCENE 3: Seidman's Place of Business. Following day.
SCENE 4: Seidman's Place of Business. One hour later.

ACT THREE

SCENE 1: Miss Menken's Apartment. Early evening, same day.
SCENE 2: Bedroom of the Seidman home. Later that evening.

The "Seidman Line" from M. Jacques Tiffeau—Monte-Sano & Pruzan Ltd.

Associate Designer to Mr. Pitkin—William Strom

Production Stage Manager—Karl Nielsen

Stage Manager—Loy Nilson

Assistant Stage Manager—Alfred Leberfeld

ix

CHARACTERS

(in order of appearance)

MORRIS SEIDMAN	Pushing fifty. As to his qualities and attributes, he will speak for himself. Volubly.
CONSTANCIA	The housekeeper.
MRS. SEIDMAN (SOPHIE)	Still an attractive woman in her forties, careful of her appearance—and of appearances.
JENNY SEIDMAN	Sixteen, unconfused and adorable.
HAROLD SEIDMAN	Twenty, confused and handsome.
DOREEN	A model.
JANICE	A seamstress.
MR. KARP	A presser with an apartment house.
ROSENZWEIG	A production man with an incipient ulcer that never burgeons.
SIDNEY	A shipping clerk with a consuming lack of ambition.
MISS WEINTRAUB	Switchboard operator. She is present only as an expressive voice.

x

LAURA MENKEN — Seidman's designer. She's a chic and attractive thirty-three. Bryn Mawr and Europe are in her background and visible in her manner and speech. She is unmarried and just beginning to be a bit worried about it.

LARRY KOGEN — Seidman's star salesman. Thirty-five, good-looking, brash but appealing; the kind of man who never needs more than one woman a night. Days, his wagon is hitched to a parimutuel star.

SHELLEY — A model.

WILENSKI — A union delegate with a soul, a social conscience and a chronically stiff neck.

LEO — A Jewish waiter. If you want further details, go get served by one.

TINA — A model.

MISS KELLEY — Mr. Magnuson's hard-bitten buyer.

MR. MAGNUSON — A hard-bitten merchant from Arkansas.

EDMAE — A model.

HELEN SOWOLSKA — Nineteen, dark, pretty, exotic-looking.

SEIDMAN AND SON

ACT ONE

Scene I

SCENE: *Dining Room of the Seidman Apartment on Central Park West, comfortably and tastefully furnished.*

AT RISE: *It's breakfast time and* MORRIS *is at the table, which is set for four. He's reading a newspaper ("Women's Wear").* CONSTANCIA, *the maid, amply proportioned, comes in from D.L. with a bowl of cooked cereal which she sets before* MORRIS.

MORRIS. [*Pours some cream from pitcher into bowl, and looks up.*] This is cream?

CONSTANCIA. [*Above table C.*] The Senora say no to use cream. Is profile milk. With powder from health store.

MORRIS. [*Puts spoon down.*] Pretty soon I'll have to have a prescription to eat breakfast here. [*Pushes bowl away.*] Make me some French toast.

CONSTANCIA. Ah, no, Senor. Is not Sunday.

MORRIS. Where is it written I can't have it on Thursday?

CONSTANCIA. I got big cleaning Thursday. Where is democracy, Senor, I stand in kitchen whole day make special breakfast?

I

[SOPHIE *enters from D.L. Her hair is done up in curlers partly concealed by a scarf tied round her head.*]

SOPHIE. What's the commotion?

MORRIS. Stop with the health foods already, Sophie. Who's got rickets?

SOPHIE. I'm sorry, Morris. What would you like for breakfast?

CONSTANCIA. Senor wishes French toast. I got busy day today. Is democracy I know night before if he [*crosses D.L.*] wishes special breakfast.

MORRIS. How do I know the night before what I'm going to want the next morning?

SOPHIE. Stancia, go make Mr. Seidman some French toast.

CONSTANCIA. [*Calamitously.*] Is fried. Fattening.

SOPHIE. Stancia—

[*She waves* CONSTANCIA *toward kitchen.* CONSTANCIA *goes out D.L.*]

MORRIS. [*As* SOPHIE *drinks her orange juice.*] She's learning very good about democracy. Pretty soon she's going to learn how to get fired in a democracy.

SOPHIE. Again fired? First you gave her lectures, she should feel free to speak her mind. So she speaks, you want to fire her. [*She goes to commode L., takes saccharine from bottle.* MORRIS *is having a hard time holding onto his injured air.*] And she happens to be right, you know. You don't need French toast. It's pure cholesterol.

MORRIS. I had a check-up last week. Happens I'm *short* cholesterol.

SOPHIE. [*Goes to* MORRIS, *kisses him.*] And temper too. Good morning, Morris. [*Takes her place at the table, drops saccharine tablet in her coffee cup.*]

MORRIS. Good morning. To you and to the hardware store in your hair.

SOPHIE. [*Patting her hair self-consciously.*] You like my hair to look nice, don't you?

MORRIS. Yeah, but for who? The ladies in your Club? All I see is curlers in the morning and curlers at night.

SOPHIE. Tell me which night you're going to come home on time for dinner, forget about the new line— so we can spend a nice evening together—and I'll be waiting for you *without* curlers in my hair.

MORRIS. You're complaining because I got a business eats me up alive?

[PHONE *on commode rings.* JENNY *enters D.L. with books which she puts on commode, picks up phone.*]

JENNY. I've got it, Ma. It's probably Marvin.

MORRIS. What's with this Marvin? We're stuck with *him* now? Morning, noon and night?

JENNY. [*Into phone.*] I'll be ready, Marvin. Just buzz —five minutes.

MORRIS. You wouldn't be ready in five minutes.

JENNY. [*Into phone.*] I can't tell you now. I'm sur- rounded. [*Throaty laugh as she listens.*] *Yes,* you goon.

[*She puts the phone down and bounds into the room. She's dressed in a sheath which sets off her lovely young figure adorably and wears a Christopher medal around her neck.*] Morning. [*Goes to* MORRIS, *kisses him, then to* SOPHIE, *gives her a kiss.*

MORRIS. I want you should sit down and have a regular breakfast.

SOPHIE. There's some cooked cereal.

JENNY. Ugh.

SOPHIE. Let's not have another commotion with *your* breakfast.

JENNY. I'm not very hungry. I'll find something. [*She runs into the kitchen.*]

MORRIS. What is that she's wearing around her neck?

SOPHIE. A Christopher medal. Marvin gave it to her.

MORRIS [*Incredulously.*]*Saint* Christopher?

SOPHIE. What then—Abe Christopher? It just means they're engaged to be engaged.

MORRIS. That's all? I'm deliriously happy it don't mean she's joining a convent.

SOPHIE. Morris, don't make a fuss. On the other side is a star of David.

MORRIS. Christopher medal with a star of David—thank God my mother isn't alive to see this.

[JENNY *comes in from the kitchen, to L. of Morris,* carrying a Coca Cola bottle and a jar of peanut butter.

Both her PARENTS *look at her with a kind of incredulous disgust.*]

MORRIS. This is breakfast? Coca Cola and peanut butter?

JENNY. Pa, I don't tell *you* what to eat.

MORRIS. [*To* JENNY.] Listen, young lady, I got a bone to pick with you. The other night at the party—[JENNY *laughs.*] What's so funny?

JENNY. Marvin is terribly impressed with you. You broke him up with that line about the twist.

SOPHIE. What did you say?

MORRIS. Nothing. I only said forty years ago we would have called it St. Vitus Dance and it would have been a tragedy for the family.

[*Enter* CONSTANCIA *D.L. with a plate of French toast, to C., above table.*]

JENNY. French toast. Ugh.

MORRIS. So where's the syrup? [CONSTANCIA *starts to protest.*] I'm warning you. If you say one word about democracy—

SOPHIE. Stancia—

MORRIS. Don't argue with her, just let her bring the syrup. [CONSTANCIA *exits D.L.*] So in front of Marvin she says to me—[*Mimicking* JENNY's *voice.* JENNY *goes to commode.*] "Pa, do me a favor, take Ma to a movie or something. The kids want to turn out the lights and make out."

[CONSTANCIA *enters with syrup and mail, puts syrup in front of* MORRIS *and crosses to* SOPHIE *with mail.*]

SOPHIE. When was this?

MORRIS. [*To* JENNY.] What do you mean you got to make out? Some expression. Where is this written? Sixteen-year-old kids. You haven't got time when you're twenty?

JENNY. [*Impishly.*] And waste four years?

[*Exit* CONSTANCIA.]

SOPHIE. Jenny! I don't like this kind of talk. [*She has picked up a manila envelope, eight by ten. She looks at the address, turns it around and tests the flap. It comes unstuck easily. To* MORRIS.] Don't eat so fast.

JENNY. [*Following across to see mail.*] What's that?

SOPHIE. For Harold.

MORRIS. So what are you opening it?

SOPHIE. It was open. It's not a letter.

JENNY. [*Craning.*] It's some kind of a magazine.

[SOPHIE *takes out the magazine, a mimeographed job, very slender.* JENNY *cranes to read the title.*] "Stars in the Purple Desk." [*Puzzled.*] Purple *desk?*

SOPHIE. [*She leafs the pages, stops, arrested by what she sees. Reading.*] "Geometry Lesson." By Harold Seidman.

JENNY. It's by Harold.

SOPHIE. [*Reads, obviously slightly bewildered.*] "Students, consider the square,

Seated upon his hypotenuse,
As in an easy chair,
Sometimes cheery, sometimes glum—"

JENNY. [*Grabs magazine, reads delightedly.*]
"But always equal to the sum
Of the adjacent squares
Who likewise say their prayers
To Winken, Blinken and Nod." [*Sits in chair to R. of* MORRIS.]

MORRIS. Let me see. [*He takes the magazine and reads.*]
"So repeat after me, students.
A straight line is, amen.
Two and two makes you know what. Amen." [*Harold enters D.L.*]
"The good man brings home the bacon.
Oh, my achin. Amen."

HAROLD. "Two good men, less the overhead, brings back a profit." [*He goes to* MORRIS, *takes the magazine from him, continues to recite.*]
"No shenanigans now, no flair,
Just stay healthy, boy,
and Square." [*Takes chair from U.R. and positions it R. of* JENNY *and sits down.*]

SOPHIE. Good morning, Harold.

HAROLD. Morning, Ma. Pa. I see somebody opened my mail.

SOPHIE. I'm sorry, darling. But the flap was open, and I couldn't resist.

HAROLD. [*Instantly mollified.*] It's okay, Ma.

MORRIS. What kind of a magazine is this, Harold? It's published by a regular company?

HAROLD. This kind of thing doesn't sell soap, Pa. It's put out by some fellows I know.

SOPHIE. Bunch of crazy beatniks.

HAROLD. Ma, I don't know any crazy beatniks. I know some fellows with ideas and talent, who want to lead their own lives—

MORRIS. You got paid something for this, Harold?

HAROLD. Is that the only yardstick, for God's sake? How much did Whitman get for *Leaves of Grass?*

MORRIS. How much?

HAROLD. I don't know, but he didn't get rich. And nobody's going to get rich from this magazine, either.

JENNY. Seems to me I've heard somewhere that achievement is more important than money.

MORRIS. Another county heard from.

SOPHIE. You'll excuse me if I think a Dr. Salk's achievement is a little greater than being published in this magazine.

HAROLD. I'd still rather have them publish my stuff than the *Saturday Evening Post.*

MORRIS. Don't worry, you won't get any argument from the *Saturday Evening Post.*

JENNY. I think it's just marvelous, Harold. Real cool. Sometime will you take a week off to explain it to me?

[HAROLD *takes a playful swipe at her. The doorbell rings.* JENNY *jumps up.*] It's Marvin.

MORRIS. He can wait five minutes.

JENNY. [*Takes her books from commode.*] I'm finished. Goodbye, you lucky parents. [*She runs out.*]

SOPHIE. Thank God we've got *one* extrovert in the family.

MORRIS. Extrovert. A new name for fresh. [HAROLD *gets up, starts out.*] Where are you going?

HAROLD. For my cigarettes. Is that all right? [*He walks out D.L. with magazine.*]

MORRIS. What is it? I could just as well be in the shop at seven o'clock. Set aside an hour to be with my family —and here we are, you, me, and Mrs. Senorita Democracy. [*Rises, crosses L.*]

SOPHIE. [*Transparently trying to lighten* MORRIS' *mood.*] It's still a family, Morris. How do you like how our Jenny looks in that sheath? Isn't that a sweet little figure that girl's got!

MORRIS. [*Crosses R. to edge of table.*] Hurts me it should be wasted on that shnook Marvin.

SOPHIE. You're just acting according to a pattern. Fathers are always jealous of their daughters' boy friends. You know Papa always hated you.

MORRIS. [*Takes cup from table, crosses to commode.*] Hated me? He hated everybody. That chicken flicker. I still remember the time I brought you home from the pictureshow five minutes late, he gave you such a crack in the face you could hear it in Yonkers. And you were eighteen, not sixteen. [*Fills coffee cup from pot on commode.*]

SOPHIE. This is one of your beautiful memories?

MORRIS. According to your modern ideas, should've been a disaster, how strict your father was. Traumas, complexes, hostilities, God knows what. So seems to me you're a pretty normal woman, a good wife, a good mother, with a nice disposition—when you are not cranky—we got yet to have our first real fight—

SOPHIE. Cranky? *Me?* [PHONE *rings.*] [*Rises, goes to phone*] Keep on, keep on, we could still have that first real fight— [SOPHIE *answers.*] Hello. [*Her expression and tone alter.*] Yes . . . One minute, please. [*Hands over phone.*] It's for Harold. The other prize—Miss Dirty-hair. [*Calls.*] Harold!

[MORRIS *resumes his seat at table.*]

HAROLD. [*From Offstage.*] Who is it?

SOPHIE. It's Miss Puswalsky.

HAROLD. [*Off.*] Sowolska, Ma. You've met her. I'll take it in here.

SOPHIE. [*Listening, hand over mouthpiece.*] Some girl he picked out.

MORRIS. [*A little malicious.*] Sophie—who's got the pattern now?

[*She hangs up, takes a seat beside* MORRIS *at table.*]

SOPHIE. Is that so? I only *pray* he would find a nice girl—

MORRIS. How do you know she's not?

SOPHIE. You saw her. Those pants. God forbid she should swallow an olive.

MORRIS. I didn't notice the pants. I was looking at the sweater. [*As* SOPHIE *flashes him a glance.*] Double cable stitch.

SOPHIE. Tell me, where do you learn this kind of humor, Morris? From your star salesman? Your models?

MORRIS. Why do you say models like I would be in some other kind of business entirely? [*Change of tone.*] What is it, Sophie? Honestly. It's *my* fault Harold quit school? Doesn't want to be a doctor—?

SOPHIE. All the time he was growing up nothing was too much for this boy. Stuffing him night and day with presents, money—if I ever said no about anything, there was always an argument in the house. Now suddenly you want him to have a sense of responsibility—

[*Rises, crosses to commode with cup, pours coffee.*] a framework of discipline—

MORRIS. Ah ha. Framework of discipline. You went to another lecture.

HAROLD. [*He enters angrily D.L.*] Helen called here last night. Couldn't you have written down the message?

SOPHIE. Who?

HAROLD. Helen Sowolska.

MORRIS. All right, kill us. We forgot to give you the message. It's not an answering service here, Harold. We got other things on our mind. [*Pause.*] Where were you all night?

HAROLD. [*Turning.*] It wasn't all night. And if you must know—I was over at Lester's place. We got talking.

MORRIS. About what, for instance?

HAROLD. About truth, for instance.

SOPHIE. [*Crosses down to R. of* MORRIS.] All night you sit around talking about truth?

HAROLD. Sleep's not the most important thing in life, Ma.

MORRIS. What is the most important thing, Harold?

HAROLD. Being awake.

MORRIS. And this you call being awake.

[SOPHIE *sits in chair R. of* MORRIS.]

HAROLD. You know, it'd be nice if you two could approve of *one* thing I do. Just one thing.

MORRIS. I'm willing, Harold. *Give* us something. Go back to college. Finish your pre-med. Or tell us at least an alternative, some kind of a plan for your life—

SOPHIE. You could have become a respected man in the community, doing important work.

HAROLD. [*Rises, drifts R.*] I know. A credit to my family.

SOPHIE. Yes. And to yourself. And you've thrown the whole thing away—for what? Tell me for what?

HAROLD. Not everybody's cut out to be a doctor, for God's sake!

SOPHIE. [*Rises.*] What are you cut out for, Harold? To be a bum—like that Lester Fineman and the rest of your wonderful friends? No plans, no ambition—look at you. Going around like a slob. This is how you expect to become a responsible man—?

HAROLD. [*Exploding.*] Ma, I'm nineteen years old. What the hell do you want from me? To sign a contract with Destiny by tomorrow morning? [*He stomps out D.L.*]

[*There's a stunned moment.*]

MORRIS. Oh, what a beautiful morning.

SOPHIE. [*Her voice catches.*] Where did we fail him, Morris? Where?

MORRIS. Why is it, with the modern psychology, it's always the parents who are failing the children? Couldn't it be sometimes that they are failing us?

SOPHIE. [*Tremulously.*] All I know is we're losing our boy. I don't recognize him any more—

MORRIS. Tomorrow he'll need his allowance, you'll recognize him. Come on, Sophie, after all, like he said—he's nineteen years old, the whole boy, let's keep a sense of proportion. Would it be better if he was brought up in back of a poultry store and had to go to work at nine years? It's so wonderful for the character—a boy growing up, dreaming all the time about a malted milk for ten cents, never having a suit except from a push-cart? What does this do for a person? Except maybe to give him bad dreams, still, at fifty? [*She looks up at him, still a little tearful but his words are having the intended effect.*] Young people are confused. It's not just now. I can remember crazy ideas *I* had—I wanted to be a violinist, a socialist, a free lover, a beachcomber. Harold will find his way too. [*Rises.*] Give him a little time. Now I got to get to the shop. I'm late. [*He kisses her cheek.*] But I'm going to have a talk with him this afternoon. From the shoulder. [*Drifts L. to commode for his hat and book of swatches.*]

SOPHIE. [*Rises, crosses to* MORRIS.] And this time, Morris—for once really put your foot down.

MORRIS. Don't worry. I'll put my foot down. Both feet.

[*The* PHONE *rings.*]

SOPHIE. [*Answers.*] Hello. Yes, darling, he's here— It's your sister. [*Hands him phone.*]

MORRIS. [*Grimaces at* SOPHIE, *takes phone.*] Yes, Bessie . . . Yes, I'm still home . . . Everybody is fine . . . Sophie is fine . . . Jenny is fine . . . Harold is fine . . . His wild ideas are also fine . . . [*His voice grows edged with irritation.*] Listen, you called me up first thing in the morning to psycho-analyze my family, or what?

SOPHIE. [*Admonishing.*] Morris.

MORRIS. [*To* SOPHIE, *his hand over the mouthpiece.*] This woman will drive me crazy. [*Into phone.*] All right, already. What else is on your mind, Mrs. Inquiring Reporter? . . . Ah-ha, the sinuses again? . . .

You got a new doctor. Use him in good health . . . Bessie, please don't take me on a conducted tour of your sinuses this morning. I got to get to the shop . . . [*Mounting exasperation.*] No, you couldn't come in for a fitting today . . . Because I am getting out the new line and nobody's got time . . . I know, I know, I'm too rich and I'm too busy for my own sister. For heaven's sake, I'll give you the money, go get yourself a dress somewhere else and drive *them* crazy. [*Bangs the phone down.*]

SOPHIE. Your own sister. You shouldn't lose your temper like that.

MORRIS. Then she shouldn't aggravate me. And don't *you* start on me now, with my temper. [SOPHIE *looks at him quizzically and he grins sheepishly, crosses R. to her.*] All right. I'll call her later and apologize. Any more instructions, Mrs. Freud?

SOPHIE. Yes. Don't wear yourself out today. [*Gives him a kiss, pulling up his coat collar.*] You'll be home for dinner?

MORRIS. If I live. If not, I'll call you. [*He exits D.L.*]

ACT ONE

SCENE II

SCENE: *Showroom of Seidman and Company later that morning.*

BEFORE RISE: *During scene change, while stage is dark, the sound of a* PHONE *is heard ringing.*

MISS WEINTRAUB'S VOICE. Seidman and Company . . . One moment, please. [*Sound of* BUZZER.] Mr. Seidman, Monarch Textiles. [*Sound of* BUZZER.] Mr. Seidman, Acme Embroidery. [*Sound of* BUZZER.] Mr. Seidman, have you time for Mr. Ogden at the bank? [*Sound of* BUZZER.] Mr. Seidman, there's somebody from Women's Wear. [*Sound of* BUZZER.] Mr. Seidman? Mr. Seidman, where are you?

MORRIS'S VOICE. I'm back here in the cutting room. For God's sake, Miss Weintraub, stop with the buzzer already. It's giving me a heartburn.

MISS WEINTRAUB'S VOICE. I'm sorry, Mr. Seidman. You want me to cut it off?

MORRIS. No. I'll just cut my head off and solve the whole problem.

MISS WEINTRAUB'S VOICE. [*Muted, aggrieved.*] Excuse me, Mr. Seidman: Excuse me for living.

16

AT RISE: LIGHTS *come up on the showroom
and* MORRIS' *office.* DOREEN *is standing in the
showroom, modelling a new number. A* FIN-
ISHER *from the shop is basting the hem.* KARP,
the presser stands by, observing. SIDNEY *walks
through, carrying some dresses, which he proceeds to hang on a rack, and exits.*

KARP. [*Admiring the dress* DOREEN *is wearing.*] Oh,
that Miss Menken. What a designer she is. When she
lays a hand on a dress—she's a genius—

[ROSENZWEIG *bursts in R. 3.*]

ROSENZWEIG. Nathan, could you stop already with the
coffee-clatching and press me out a few dresses? I got
orders to fill, a new line to get out, I got the union
delegate coming in—

KARP. What do you think I got here, Rosie, a pressing
machine or a sausage machine? Install a set of buttons
on my head—

ROSENZWEIG. Don't give me ideas. Just give me samples.
Period. End of paragraph. [KARP *exits L. 2, while*
SIDNEY *enters R 3, pushing a handcart of material.*]
You. Mr. Fireball from the shipping department. What
are you dragging here?

SIDNEY. I'm not dragging, Mr. Rosenzweig, I'm pushing.

ROSENZWEIG. Comedians too, I got. Everything but an
organization to get me out a few dresses. What are you
pushing?

SIDNEY. [*Handing him a bill.*] Embroidery from Acme.
For Miss Menken.

ROSENZWEIG. I knew it, sooner or later she would order behind my back. Take it back to the shipping room.

SIDNEY. What should I do with it?

ROSENZWEIG. I'll tell you in a minute what you should do with it. Take it back and don't give me any arguments. A designer she calls herself.

[ROSENZWEIG *exits L. 2 and* SIDNEY *exits R. 3. The* BUZZER *in the showroom sounds.*]

DOREEN. [*Answering it.*] Yes.

MISS WEINTRAUB'S VOICE. Miss Menken?

DOREEN. One minute, Miss Weintraub—[*Calling off.*] Miss Menken—

[MISS MENKEN *enters L. 2 with pattern.*]

DOREEN. Call for you.

MISS MENKEN. Thank you, Doreen. [*Pressing button on phone.*] Yes, Miss Weintraub.

MISS WEINTRAUB'S VOICE. Mr. Seidman wants the pattern for six-three-eight. He's at the cutting table.

MISS MENKEN. Tell him I'm sending it right back. [*Calls.*] Janice. [JANICE *enters R. 3.* MISS MENKEN *hands the pattern to* JANICE *who exits with it R. 3.*] Oh, and Miss Weintraub, would you tell Mr. Seidman the samples are ready now for Harpers Bazaar and need his approval?

MISS WEINTRAUB'S VOICE. Yes, Miss Menken.

[LARRY KOGEN *enters L. 2.*]

LARRY. Morning, Miss Menken. Morning, Doreen.

MISS MENKEN. Why, Mr. Kogen—

LARRY. You're looking great this morning. Cool and luscious, like a lime parfait.

MISS MENKEN. Mr. Kogen, it was so peaceful here while you were away on the road. Couldn't you be induced to take another trip?

LARRY. Ah, come on, Miss Menken. You know you missed me.

MISS MENKEN. Oh, we all missed you, Mr. Kogen. It was wonderful.

LARRY. Well, I missed *you*. It's good to come back to that warm, smiling face of yours.

MISS MENKEN. And start heckling me about the line.

LARRY. That's different. Business is business. [*Back to the dress.*] Now—what have we here? You still on that Etruscan kick? [*He reaches for* DOREEN.] Pull your stomach in, baby. That dress'll look better.

[MORRIS *enters R. 3.*]

MORRIS. Larry! What are *you* doing in the shop. There's no horses running today?

LARRY. I'm watching the birth of a new era in the dress business. Etruscan Modern. Very fascinating.

MISS MENKEN. Mr. Seidman, do you have time now to approve the accessories on the samples before they are sent out to be photographed.

MORRIS. Of course.

MISS MENKEN. [*Calls.*] Shelley.

[SHELLEY *enters in a red and black dress.*]

MORRIS. That's very striking, Miss Menken. For the photograph be sure to have her wear the long black gloves.

MISS MENKEN. Right. [*Calls.*] Tina. [TINA *enters in a green check suit.*] The check wool suit.

MORRIS. This is the one with the cowl?

MISS MENKEN. Yes, I have it right here. [*She hands it* to TINA *to put on.*]

MORRIS. Yes, I prefer that to the hood.

MISS MENKEN. Thank you, Tina. [TINA *exits.*] Doreen. [DOREEN *enters in the Etruscan Modern number.*] This is the Etruscan Modern.

MORRIS. Beautiful. Beautiful! I predict this is going to be one of our big numbers this season.

LARRY. Aw, come on, Miss Menken, these dresses are great for New York and Palm Beach, but Morris, in Boise, Idaho, I'm going to have to sell them with a set of dishes. I got a fixed idea in my stupid head that a dress ought to make a woman look like a woman. [*Crosses to* DOREEN, *grabs a handful of the dress in back.* DOREEN *shies.*] Hold still, baby, this won't hurt a bit. [*He holds the dress tight, outlining her bust.*] What's wrong with putting a belt on it, at least?

MISS MENKEN. Only that it ruins the line of the dress, and is completely against the style trend of all the leading designers this season.

LARRY. Oh, the hell with the leading designers. Ninety percent of them hate women. How do you sell a dress like this to a girl who weighs a hundred and thirty-five pounds? They've got to live, too.

[BOSENZWEIG *enters aflame, L. 2, carrying a box of buttons.*]

ROSENZWEIG. Miss Menken. Did you order these?

MISS MENKEN. Yes, Mr. Rosenzweig, I did. For seven-oh-six. [*She scornfully crosses past him Upstage.*]

ROSENZWEIG. [*Turns to* MORRIS, *anguished.*] On my bended knees—I am the production man here; this is my function—tell her to check with me before she orders. Otherwise, send me to a sanitarium—one of the two.

MORRIS. Stop with the sanitarium. I'll be there long before you. I don't understand. You're a man lived through two wars and four Republican administrations. If the buttons are not right—throw them away and order another gross. Everything has to be a crisis with you?

ROSENZWEIG. [*Abashed.*] You're right, Morris. I'm sorry.

[MORRIS *exits into his office as the* BUZZER *sounds.*]

MISS WEINTRAUB'S VOICE. Mr. Rosenzweig. Superior Button Company returning your call.

ROSENZWEIG. [*Picks up phone; his tone is very reasonable now.*] Mr. Superior Button Company? . . . Yes, I called you. [*Suddenly and uncontrollably exploding.*] I'll tell you what it is. The superior buttons you sent me this morning, you're going to get the whole thing back in your face. . . . No, they are not right, they

are cockeyed, lopsided and besides I didn't order them
and next time you'll check with me before you take an
order here or I will get myself another button company.
You are not the only button company on the beach.
Period. End of paragraph. [*He slams the receiver down.*
SIDNEY *has entered R. 3 during above, carrying some
swatches; he stands waiting, in an attitude of expectant
terror.*]

MORRIS. [*Sticks his head into showroom; his tone is
half amused, half exasperated.*] Rosenzweig—[ROSEN-
ZWEIG *turns to him, gestures helpless apology for his
burst of temper; he turns away, sees* SIDNEY *and again,
uncontrollably, blows a fuse.*]

ROSENZWEIG. You: Mr. Guided Missile from the shipping department. What are you standing there with
your mouth open?

SIDNEY. You asked me to bring you these swatches—

ROSENZWEIG. So what took you so long? [*They* BOTH
exit L. 2.]

MISS MENKEN. [*Crossing into* MORRIS' *office through
R. 2.*] Mr. Seidman, can any one be expected to work
in this atmosphere? All this interference.

MORRIS. [*Placatingly.*] Miss Menken, don't get upset.
You'll get used to the atmosphere here. We got a production manager sometimes acts like he would be on
the stage of the Metropolitan Opera House—and a star
salesman who's got nothing but mating on his brain—
but otherwise, it's a pretty normal establishment. You
got only one person you got to please around here. And
I am very pleased with your work. I got every confi-

dence in you. We are going to have a great line this season. Go. Create.

MISS MENKEN. Thank you, Mr. Seidman. Come on, Doreen. [*Followed by* DOREEN, MISS MENKEN *exits U.L.* LARRY *gives* DOREEN *a pat on the behind.*]

MORRIS. [*Going into his office.*] Larry!

LARRY. What?

DOREEN. You'll get a hand chopped off one of these days. [*Exits R. 2.*]

LARRY. [*Follows* MORRIS *into office.*] She's really got it, that Doreen. She does something for a dress.

MORRIS. [*Looking up now.*] Larry, somebody could look into your head, they would see only three things— a racing form, a deck of cards, and a patented brassiere comes off with a look.

LARRY. I got something else in my head, Morris. A picture of myself sitting behind a desk like yours, some- day, sending some other rag peddler to Boise, Idaho, and Medicine Hat, Wyoming.

MORRIS. So what do you want from me? Get yourself a designer and start up for yourself. I'll send you con- gratulations for the opening. But for now don't start up with Miss Menken, making her nervous. It cost me a fortune to hire her away from Vanity Frocks and I didn't take her for her looks. She's got a wonderful background, the best references, she won prizes for her designs in Paris—

LARRY. I know, I know. And she's got a diploma from Bryn Mawr, and she sleeps in double percale sheets that she keeps crisp in the refrigerator. What she needs, for my money, is a long steamy weekend in Miami Beach to thaw out.

MORRIS. This I don't think you could swing with Miss Menken.

LARRY. Why don't *you* put in a little overtime with her, Boss? I think she kinda goes for you.

MORRIS. Larry, you got plenty opportunities for your humor—politics, religion, minorities—

LARRY. Come on, Morris. Level. You've been married twenty-five years. Vanilla, vanilla—don't you ever get tired of it? A little strawberry sometimes. Pistachio?

MORRIS. Listen, I'll make you a speech, and I want you should remember it. I got a certain feeling about marriage. Like a fine piece of velvet. One time you drop it in the dirt, finished. You could clean it, clean it, never the same. I am not telling anybody else how to live. They should only live and be well. But this little territory you are going to leave alone with your jokes, you understand me?

LARRY. [*Shaking his head, with a grin.*] Morris, either you're the biggest faker that ever lived—or you belong in a book.

MORRIS. I'm in a book. Dun and Bradstreet. I'd like to be a big hero there, with a triple-A rating. [INTERCOM *buzzes.* MORRIS *answers.*]

MISS WEINTRAUB'S VOICE. Mr. Wilenski from the Union is here, Mr. Seidman. He and Mr. Rosenzweig have gone into the showroom.

MORRIS. I'll be right there.

MISS WEINTRAUB'S VOICE. There's a call for you. Somebody from the Health Department.

MORRIS. Health Department? [*Picks up phone.*] Hello
. . . Yes, this is Mr. Seidman . . . You got a complaint from a Mr. Sowalska, what has that got to do
with me? . . . Oh, my son? Well, he couldn't sign on
a complaint, he's a minor . . . I don't know what it's
all about. If you'll send it here, I'll look into it. [*He
hangs up, and rises to go.*] Health Department?

LARRY. Morris, if that was my boy, I wouldn't let him
flounder around. You got a gold mine here—

MORRIS. He doesn't need a gold mine. He needs a life
with some dignity. Some meaning to it.

LARRY. Morris, sometimes you're a complete enigma to
me.

MORRIS. I wish I could return the compliment. [*Exits
into shop.* WILENSKI, *the union delegate, and* ROSEN-
ZWEIG, *enter the showroom from L. 2.*] Hello, Wilenski. You're not going to make me any trouble, now?

WILENSKI. Trouble? All I'm asking is a fair price for
your workers.

MORRIS. Sure. All you're ever asking is a fair price. And
for you a fair price is the retail price of the dress, plus
a bonus, two weeks' vacation, and I should throw in
my stocks and insurance policies besides. Come in, Tina.
[TINA *enters L. 2, modeling a dress.* MORRIS *sits chair
R.*] So what's with this dress? Number six-fourteen.
Simple little number—

WILENSKI. [*Examining dress.*] Some simple. You got on this dress pleating, a yoke, five seams—

ROSENZWEIG & MORRIS. [*In concert.*] Four seams.

WILENSKI. Five seams I count.

ROSENZWEIG. [*Screaming.*] What are you telling me five seams? It's four seams!

MORRIS. Rosenzweig, control yourself.

ROSENZWEIG. How could I control myself when a man tells me five seams? I laid out the pattern myself. What am I, a production man or an idiot? Control myself he says. Everybody around here could have temperament —designers, union delegates, bosses, salesmen—only me, I got to have an adjusted personality.

[*During above* MORRIS *and* WILENSKI *have settled themselves into attitudes of resignation, waiting for the accustomed tornado to pass.*]

WILENSKI. [*Looking significantly at his watch.*] All right Rosenzweig. You're finished? [*Turns to* MORRIS.] Four seams, five seams, I figure this dress got to cost nine-fifty for the operating.

MORRIS. [*Screaming.*] Nine-fifty? Before I pay you even eight dollars, I'll throw the dress out of the line altogether.

WILENSKI. Go ahead. You'll be doing the operators a favor. A dress like this got to take an operator a whole day.

ROSENZWEIG. For what, a whole day? To check on their real estate maybe?

MORRIS. Rosenzweig, go check on your own real estate. *I'll* handle this.

WILENSKI. Mr. Seidman—it's not a nuclear equation we got to figure out here. We're reasonable men. You got here at least three yards piping.

MORRIS & ROSENZWEIG. [*Together.*] A yard and a half.

WILENSKI. All right, why should we argue? Let's measure. [*Produces tape and crosses to* TINA, *U.C.*]

ROSENZWEIG. Not with your tape measure from Las Vegas. Use mine.

[INTERCOM *buzzes.* MORRIS *rises and crosses to phone as they measure the piping.*]

MORRIS. [*Presses phone button.*] Yes.

MISS WEINTRAUB'S VOICE. Mr. Seidman, have you got time for the shop foreman?

MORRIS. No. Not now— [*Releases button.*]

WILENSKI. So it's two and a half yards piping. Figure nine and a quarter—

MORRIS. All right, Rosenzweig, we could forget about this number.

[ROSENZWEIG. *takes* TINA *by the arm, and starts to drag her out.* MORRIS *drags her back.*]

MORRIS. Eight dollars, eight dollars, or the dress is out of the line. [*D.L.*]

WILENSKI. [*Crosses to* MORRIS.] Mr. Seidman, where is your conscience? Why do I have to have with you such arguments? Your workers are entitled to a life, too—to give their children an education—

MORRIS. Listen to me, Mr. Graduate-from-the-Labor-Relations-School; you'll go on making my life a misery; I can't put out a dress to make a decent profit—I'll close my doors altogether, and go to Florida. Raise oranges. [*Sits chair L.*]

WILENSKI. You think you'll be happier, squeezing oranges instead of workers?

MORRIS. Eight-fifty. That's more than the dress is worth.

WILENSKI. Nine dollars. And you are getting away with murder.

ROSENZWEIG. Look who's talking about Murder. Wilenski, the Ripper.

MORRIS. Rosenzweig, stop helping me already.

WILENSKI. [*To* MORRIS.] From him, I don't want any insults. I'll walk.

MORRIS. [*Rises, crossing R.*] Walk. Run. Eight seventy-five. This is my last word.

WILENSKI. All right. Eight seventy-five. [WILENSKI *and* MORRIS *shake hands. And suddenly the three sit in relief;* WILENSKI *D.L.,* MORRIS *U.L.,* ROSENZWEIG *R.* TINA *exits L. 2.*]

MORRIS. [*After a breather.*] Well, how's Libby?

WILENSKI. Fine, fine. [*Remembering.*] She said to ask Sophie if you could come for dinner next Saturday night.

MORRIS. Why not? We'll maybe have a little pinochle after.

WILENSKI. What then? [*Grimacing, as he gives his head a twist.*] Maybe I could still get to the Turkish Bath. My neck is killing me.

ROSENZWEIG. Wait till tonight, I'll go with you.

WILENSKI. Tonight I can't. I got tickets to the opera.

MORRIS. It's *Tosca* tonight, no? With Tebaldi?

WILENSKI. Yeah.

MORRIS. I hear she's great. But for me, the greatest Tosca was Mary Garden.

ROSENZWEIG. My barber says the greatest of all was Tetrazzini.

WILENSKI. You got to get yourself a new barber. Happens Tetrazzini was a coloratura. She never played Tosca in her whole life. And besides, he gave you a rotten haircut the last time.

[INTERCOM *buzzes.*]

ROSENZWEIG. [*Answers.*] Yes?

MISS WEINTRAUB'S VOICE. Mr. Seidman, your son is here.

MORRIS. Tell him to wait.

ROSENZWEIG. [*To intercom.*] Tell him to wait.

MISS WEINTRAUB'S VOICE. And Mr. Rosenzweig is wanted in the shop.

ROSENZWEIG. I'll be right there. [*He hurries out R. 3.*]

MORRIS. [*Rises, crosses to* WILENSKI; *they shake*

hands.] Well, goodbye, Mr. Wilenski. Enjoy yourself at the opera. You'll see there plenty of your exploited working class. Me, I got to stay in my shop and figure out how to make a living.

WILENSKI. [*Rises.*] You are breaking my heart, Mr. Seidman. [*Mutters.*] Nine dollars for a dress like this— [*Exits L.*]

MORRIS. [*Yelling.*] Eight seventy-five. And don't forget it.

[WILENSKI *exits L. 2.* MORRIS *starts for office, from L. 2,* LARRY *enters, leading* DOREEN *who is wearing a striking, but extreme-looking dress.*]

LARRY. [*Heatedly, crossing D. L.*] Look, Morris, this is what I mean. Sure it's striking—it's stunning. But who's going to wear it—a female gladiator? Are we out to sell some dresses to our regular trade this season, or win an Oscar for cockeyed design?

[MISS MENKEN *has stormed in L. 2 during the last of* LARRY'S *speech.* DOREEN *drifts Upstage.*]

MISS MENKEN. Mr. Seidman, I can't go on this way any longer. Every time I turn around, there's somebody neglecting his own job to tell me what I'm supposed to do.

MORRIS. Miss Menken—

MISS MENKEN [*Continuing heatedly.*] I want something understood around here. You're paying me a lot of money to get your line out. Either I'm going to be allowed to do it without interference, or I'm quitting as of now.

MORRIS. Miss Menken, you are not quitting. [*To* DOREEN.] Thank you, Doreen. [DOREEN *exits L. 2.*] I have a contract with you, and if you break it, I'll see to it you won't work anywhere in this industry, I promise you. Now go back to work.

MISS MENKEN. All right, Mr. Seidman. But you know what my conditions are. And I particularly want you to impress them on that dime-store Casanova of yours.

[*She exits L. 2.*]

MORRIS. [*Crossing to* LARRY.] Listen, Mr. Star Salesman, I'm telling you for the last time to stop mixing in with the line. When the line is finished, you'll sell it. And if you can't sell it, you'll go somewhere next season where they make better styles. I'll give you a recommendation. [*Starts for his office.*]

[*During this speech,* HAROLD *comes into* MORRIS' *office through R. 1. Seeing his* FATHER *busy in the showroom, he waits.*]

LARRY. Morris, listen—

MORRIS. [*Turns toward* LARRY.] What do you think I am? Some kind of a teddy bear or something, you can throw around, play games? Now, get out!

LARRY. Temper, Temper. [LARRY *exits L. 2.*]

[MORRIS *goes into his office, sees* HAROLD *standing L. of desk.*]

MORRIS. Oh—Harold—

HAROLD. Hi, Pa. Ma said you wanted to talk to me.

MORRIS. Yes. What's with you and the Health Department.

HAROLD. How did you find out?

MORRIS. They called up. You got to sign on a complaint?

HAROLD. It's the Sowalskas. The father was a pharmacist over in Poland—but he can't get a license here.

MORRIS. So?

HAROLD. You should see how they live, five of them crowded in a one-bedroom flat. The plaster is falling off the ceilings, the plumbing doesn't work, there hasn't been an exterminator around there in a year. So I went to have a talk with the landlord. You know what he said? Go back and tell them they're two months behind in the rent.

MORRIS. Well, it's too bad, Harold. But he's the landlord. It's not unreasonable he should want his rent.

HAROLD. Oh, I knew you'd be on his side.

MORRIS. I'm not on anybody's side. I don't think you'll accomplish anything with the Health Department. They should go to some refugee organization— [*Sits down at his desk*]

HAROLD. They've been all through that. They're scared to death to complain about anything. Don't you understand? Where they come from, a complaint is as good as a death warrant.

MORRIS. Well, I don't think you should mix in—

HAROLD. For God's sake, somebody's got to care what happens to people. Not just sit around saying don't mix in. That's just what the landlord said.

MORRIS. [*Rises, crosses L.*] So your solution is the landlord should give them a bigger apartment for free.

And if you'll get the A and P to give them groceries on the same basis—

HAROLD. [*Crosses in to* MORRIS.] Excuse me for forgetting that profits are more important than human values.

MORRIS. What's the matter? Profit is a dirty word with you suddenly? You've been living pretty good for nineteen years on my profits.

HAROLD. Yeah. I agree with you. Maybe it's time I got off.

MORRIS [*Looks at him for a moment.*] Sit down, Harold.

HAROLD. I can hear you just as well, standing.

MORRIS. [*Sits down himself, heavily, on bench L.*] What is it, Harold? Suddenly I'm your enemy. You can't trust me any more, you can't talk to me, like a person.

HAROLD. Pa, I want to talk to you. But you won't listen. You tuned me out the minute I said I didn't want to be a doctor. Nothing I can say to you seems to matter. [*Pleading.*] Pa, maybe I wasn't supposed to get the Nobel Prize for medicine. Maybe I'm supposed to be just another clamshell turning over on the bottom of the ocean.

MORRIS. To be a clamshell? This is your ambition.

HAROLD. Yes. If you want to put it that way. To be quiet and simple. To make long lists of all the things I don't need, that scream and claw at you every place you turn—the houses and furniture and cars—

MORRIS. Wait a minute, Harold. I gave up a good part of my life to get these things for my family.

HAROLD. Maybe you gave up too much—

MORRIS. What I gave up is why you can afford to be so choosy?

HAROLD. What's the use of this, Pa? We just don't speak the same language any more.

MORRIS. [*Flaring.*] Well, let me tell you something. You better go back to the old language or learn a new language! [HAROLD *starts for the door.*] Wait a minute. You're serious about this writing business?

HAROLD. I'm serious.

MORRIS. All right, you want a chance to prove yourself? You've got an allowance, sit home and write.

HAROLD. [*Comes toward* MORRIS; *his tone now pleads for understanding.*] Don't you see, it won't work. It may take me five years, or ten to get anything published—and then it's not likely to be up there on the best seller list.

MORRIS. You think this is all that matters to me? [*Crosses D.L.*]

HAROLD. I don't know. You asked me this morning how much I got paid for that hunk of verse.

MORRIS. [*Rises and crosses to* HAROLD.] What's the matter, Hemingway didn't get paid for writing? Somerset Maugham bought his art collection with green stamps? Tell the truth, Harold, you really want to be a writer? Or a bum with a high-class excuse?

HAROLD. All right, Pa. I want to be a bum with a high-class excuse.

MORRIS. [*Exploding.*] Don't close up on me. I'm talking to you about your life. How will you live? On what?

HAROLD. [*Turning away, L.*] I'll make out somehow.

MORRIS. [*Crossing to* HAROLD.] You are talking so much about the world and it's like you would be living— I don't know where. On Mars. What could you do? You got no experience. What could you get? A messenger job, a laboring job. You know what you'll earn? To take home, maybe thirty-eight dollars a week. You'll want to have a place of your own—so the least you could expect to pay for a room, shouldn't be full of cockroaches, is ten dollars a week. Cheap meals got to cost you, minimum four dollars a day, say twenty-five dollars a week. Clothing three dollars a week, laundry, cleaning, cigarettes, dates, and a movie, fifteen dollars a week. So that's fifty dollars. Already you are behind twelve dollars.

HAROLD. [*A bit sheepishly.*] I've got like a problem, haven't I? [*Sits on bench, L.*]

MORRIS. You want to be sensible, Harold? I got a proposition for you. You need a job, I could use a bright young man. [*Sits on bench beside* HAROLD.]

HAROLD. What could I do here? I don't want to take anybody else's job—

MORRIS. [*Humorously.*] Don't be foolish. You don't know enough to take anybody else's job here, not even a shipping clerk's. But you could learn. It's not what I dreamed for you, Harold. But what I was dreaming, you don't want. But listen, it doesn't have to be so bad. Maybe you'll get to like the business— [*Again, humorously as he sees* HAROLD's *expression.*] As a sideline, I mean. Maybe someday we'll put up a sign, Seidman and Son, and we'd have, like Dupont, a dynasty going.

HAROLD. [*Laughs.*] Ah, Pa.

MORRIS. What's the matter? Only the Gentiles can merge?

HAROLD. Pa, if I did come to work here, you've got to understand it's not a career for me. I want to write.

MORRIS. So write, Saturdays, Sundays, nights—if you want to. Better than if you would be working in a garage. You got your own room, nobody will bother you. I'll tell Rosenzweig to put you on the payroll tomorrow, all right? You want to wait a couple minutes, I'll go home with you. [*Rises, goes to his desk.*]

HAROLD. [*Rises, goes to door R. 2.*] I'm not going right home. I'll be home later.

MORRIS. What about dinner?

HAROLD. Don't worry, Pa, I'll eat.

MORRIS. [*Goes to* HAROLD *at door.*] Listen, Harold, do me one favor. [*Draws him back into office with an arm around his shoulder.*] When you talk to your mother about coming in to the shop—you don't have to tell her all this business of it's not a career and so on. Show a little enthusiasm, so she'll think it's some kind of substitute at least for not becoming Dr. Salk. Know what I mean? I got to live with her too.

HAROLD. Okay, Pa. [*He exits through showroom and off L. 2.*]

MORRIS. [*Turns to his desk, switches on the* INTERCOM.] Miss Weintraub, get me my house. And tell Miss Menken I would like to see her. [*He picks up the phone, takes a swallow of water.* BUZZER *sounds. Into phone.*] Hello, Sophie . . . Yes, he was here. We had a good talk . . . Look, everything is not solved yet but at least he's coming to work in the shop in the morning . . . I'll tell you all about it when I get home . . . What's for dinner . . . [*Vegetable* dinner? . . . This is what I worked myself up to? [MISS MENKEN *enters, dispirited. She stands hesitantly in the showroom.*] I'll be home when I'm finished . . . Sophie, I'm not a train, I don't run on a schedule . . . When I'll be home, I'll be home . . . I'll see you later [*He hangs up.*]

MISS MENKEN. [*At office door.*] Did you want to see me, Mr. Seidman?

MORRIS. Yes. You got an appointment? I'm not keeping you?

MISS MENKEN. [*Turns back into showroom as* MORRIS *follows her.*] No.

MORRIS. Sit down for a minute. I didn't call you in to talk to you about the line. [MISS MENKEN *sits stiffly in a chair, U.L.C.,* MORRIS *stands R. of her.*] It's on my conscience that I hollered on you.

MISS MENKEN. Please don't concern yourself about my feelings, Mr. Seidman. I'm here to design a line of dresses.

MORRIS. Your feelings are just as important to me as the dresses.

MISS MENKEN. Mr. Seidman, maybe I'm not the right person for this job.

MORRIS. Please, Miss Menken. You got no reason to be so upset.

MISS MENKEN. Of course not. I'm just another machine around here, for producing designs. I'm not supposed to react. Just use up my ration of chalk and pins every day, get screamed at and trampled on by everybody in the place.

MORRIS. So I lost my temper [*Soothing.*] It wasn't against you, personal. I got a lot on my mind these days.

MISS MENKEN. [*Responding.*] It isn't you, Mr. Seidman. If it weren't for you around here I'd really be lost.

MORRIS. [*Brightly.*] So why don't we go down to Manny's Blue Room, we'll have a bite and you'll tell me all about it, you'll feel better. Yes?

MISS MENKEN. [*Rises.*] It's a kind offer but I'm afraid I wouldn't know where to start.

MORRIS. Well, we'll start with a little appetizer—[*Goes into his office for his hat and jacket which is hung on a dress dummy at upper right wall.*] then some soup, maybe some roast chicken—

MISS MENKEN. Really, Mr. Seidman—

MORRIS. [*Returns to showroom putting on coat and hat.*] Who's the boss? [*Goes to her.*] Come on, fix yourself up a little, they shouldn't think in Manny's we're having trouble here. You know how rumors start flying on Seventh Avenue. Somebody will see you upset, right away they'll think we're having trouble with the line—[*Takes her arm, starts toward door.*] going to have a bad season, going to lose money, maybe with one more bad season I'll be broke, why wait, chop off the credit now. Then I'll start to cry and from this could come a flood altogether. [MISS MENKEN *is laughing.*]

MISS MENKEN. Mr. Seidman, I do appreciate all this. But really—I'm not a mental case—

MORRIS. Wait, Miss Menken, wait.

[*They exit, D.L., both laughing.*]

CURTAIN

ACT TWO

Scene I

Scene: *Manny's Blue Room. Early evening. Same day.*

At Rise: morris *and* miss menken *are seated at a table,* morris *L. of* miss menken. leo *attends them.* leo *is a Jewish waiter, which is to say that for a modest tip he will serve as physician, Dutch uncle and mentor, as well as waiter.*

leo. [*Enters from U.R. to L. of* miss menken *and sets down a drink for her.*] What's with a little nourishment, we shouldn't float away entirely?

morris. Do me a favor, Leo, float away yourself. All right, bring us some chopped liver. The rest I'll tell you later.

[leo *exits.*]

miss menken. You shouldn't worry about your son. He seems pretty stable.

morris. All of a sudden we don't speak the same language.

miss menken. I wouldn't take that too seriously. I can remember saying that to *my* parents. Can't you?

MORRIS. No, we all spoke the same language—"What's going to be with the rent?" I suppose it's maybe comical how we are making a fuss, our kind of people, immigrants, about a son becoming a doctor or a lawyer —a respected member of the community.

MISS MENKEN. No, I understand, but successful writers lead very rewarding lives.

MORRIS. Sure. A Tolstoy, a Balzac, a Victor Hugo— this would be wonderful. But what do I see with the modern writing? Knock down everything, criticize everything—or else it's only about dope addicts, sex maniacs, perverts—[*With a helpless shrug.*] I don't know. I guess I got my ideas fixed in another time. What a dream we had about America in those days. It wasn't just the gold in the streets like everybody said. I always tried to improve myself. [LEO *enters R. with another drink and some chopped liver, which he serves during the following.*] I remember those little blue books for a nickel. It was a lot of money in those days. A nickel. But what you *got* for it! Socrates, Emerson, Voltaire—

LEO. Elbert Hubbard—

[MORRIS *gives him a look.* LEO *withers and exits R.*]

MORRIS. But what about the young people today—what are their dreams? What have they got respect for? They are not bad children, don't misunderstand me—but from where is going to come the beauty, the romance—a little genuine emotion in their lives? From the television? The movies? Seriously. Could you find one time a little genuine feeling between a man and a woman? Either they're making from sex some kind of a joke, or else it's a war going on between a man and a woman, when they come together finally for a kiss, on the big screen their mouths look a half a block long, you could see the tongues, like from a cow, this is not love any more, this is delicatessen. [MISS MENKEN *laughs.*] No I mean it, what happened to sentiment in the world, Miss Menken? Like they called it in my old days. "The Tender Passion."

MISS MENKEN. Now, you don't go back *that* far.

MORRIS. Sometimes I feel like I'm from the year one. But I got you down here on false pretenses. We were going to talk about *your* problems.

MISS MENKEN. I think you're a very devious man, Mr. Seidman. And a very nice one. [*She smiles at him warmly, swallows the rest of her drink.*]

MORRIS. Have a little chopped liver?

[*She nods. He spreads some of the liver on a piece of rye bread, hands it to her. She puts it on her plate, abstracted.*]

MISS MENKEN. That lovely phrase. "The tender passion." Calls up a whole era.

[*A moment of silence between them, filled with growing awareness of each other.* LEO *enters* R. MISS MENKEN *holds up her empty glass.* LEO *gives* MORRIS *a significant glance.*]

LEO. Nu?

MORRIS. Leo, don't be such a nag. I got enough guardians at home. [LEO *exits.*] Miss Menken, we got to form in the shop, a United Nations you and me. First of all, about Rosenzweig. If he upsets you, I'm still the boss, you could always come to me.

MISS MENKEN. You heard that explosion today over seven-oh-six. I don't like to come running to you with every problem, twenty times a day—

MORRIS. Remind me—what is seven-oh-six? Oh yes, this is the one with the embroidery, you copied from Balenciaga. Excuse me, I didn't mean *copied* from Balenciaga. I mean you were *inspired* by Balenciaga.

MISS MENKEN. You're very cute, Mr. Seidman. Has anyone ever told you?

MORRIS. I can't remember. But it doesn't hurt to hear it again. It's not like a notice in bankruptcy. [LEO *enters R. with her drink, sets it down before her and departs, exuding disapproval.*] It's a good drink, that vodka gimlet? [*She holds out her glass for him to taste; he takes a sip.*] Mmm, very nice, I haven't got much of a taste for drinking but sometimes I got to go out with Larry and a customer—

MISS MENKEN. I don't think this would suit Mr. Kogen. A baseball bat in a glass is more his style.

MORRIS. Actually, you know, I don't think he is much of a drinker either. He's got other accomplishments.

MISS MENKEN. Really, Mr. Seidman, I couldn't care less about Mr. Kogen's "accomplishments."

MORRIS. I seen women who should know a lot better— hard-boiled buyers, models—lose their heads over Larry.

MISS MENKEN. Well, I find him quite resistible. That deceptively boyish air of his—he must be forty-five—

MORRIS. He's thirty-four. Going on forty-five.

MISS MENKEN [*Reacts, then.*] I'd just love to teach that man a lesson. I really would.

MORRIS. Miss Menken—take my advice. You're looking for a little excitement, take up parachute jumping, shark hunting, sky writing. Don't give Larry Kogen lessons.

MISS MENKEN. You're right, Mr. Seidman, I know I'm not fooling you. [*The look she gives him now is troubled, vulnerable.*] Why is it the *bad* boys always attract me? I should have learned by now that I'm not going to change them, be a good influence—I just end up getting hurt. [*Shakes her head.*] Sounds kind of sick, sick, doesn't it?

MORRIS. Stop with the sick. You're human, that's all. You're a very honest, decent woman. Besides lovely. That's all I could say.

MISS MENKEN. [*She bends forward impulsively, puts her hand on his, then removes it self-consciously.*] Thank you. [*She swallows the last of her drink.*] I really should go. I don't do this very often. You've been very patient.

MORRIS. I'm selfish. I got to look after the best designer I ever had.

MISS MENKEN. Please don't spoil me. I'm not used to so much consideration. I've got to go home now—my Siamese cat is waiting for me.

MORRIS. Let me get you something to eat, and for your cat we'll get a knish.

MISS MENKEN. [*Smiles, then again, impulsively.*] May I tell you something, Mr. Seidman? I'm a little drunk so I can say it. You're somebody very special. Very special indeed.

MORRIS. Put something in your stomach. You'll feel better.

MISS MENKEN. I've embarrassed you.

MORRIS. Not embarrassed. But you are a very attractive woman, Miss Menken. And even at my age—

MISS MENKEN. Your age? Why you're a vigorous man, in the prime of life.

MORRIS. I could stand some exercise, believe me. I'm soft, like a tapioca.

MISS MENKEN. I don't know how you wandered into this jungle. You're kind and generous—and most of all you have an understanding heart. Promise me you won't ever lose it.

MORRIS. If I promise, will you eat something?

[LEO *comes in, R. eyeing* MISS MENKEN *as if she were something in a cage, crosses to* MORRIS.]

LEO [*Sotto Voce.*] I got a regards for you. From Table 14. The Roselles.

MORRIS. Thank you. You could tell them to stop watching like we would be a floor show. Bring us some sturgeon— [LEO *brightens visibly.*] Nice thick slices. With some sweet red peppers. And for the lady another vodka gimlet. [*With decision.*] And bring me a drink also.

LEO. Celery tonic or plain.

MORRIS. No, I mean a drink. A vodka gimlet.

LEO. [*Looking up from his order pad, aghast.*] You're starting now?

CURTAIN

ACT TWO

Scene II

Scene: *The* seidman *bedroom. Several hours later.*

At Rise: sophie *is in bed, reading, her hair is done up in curlers.* morris *enters from D.L. wearing street clothes as in last scene. His manner at the beginning of the scene is jaunty, but this soon fades.*

morris. [*L. of bed.*] Again curlers? [*As she turns a page, ignoring him.*] Where is the beautiful Sophie Frisch I married? You are always hiding her behind those irons in your hair.

sophie. Don't act as if it made any difference to you.

morris. [*Sits down on L. side of bed.*] What's the matter, Sophie? You're in a mood tonight?

sophie. I thought you were coming home early. For dinner.

morris. I'm sorry. Kill me. Something came up.

sophie. What about Harold? You were going to tell me what happened.

morris. He didn't tell you?

sophie. No.

MORRIS. Well, like I told you on the phone—he's coming to work in the place.

SOPHIE. He's definitely not going back to school?

MORRIS. No. He doesn't want the Nobel Prize for medi·cine. Do him something?

SOPHIE. So he'll be a dress man—a rich, cultural life. Larry Kogen, models—

MORRIS. Models he could meet without being a dress man. Don't worry. He could have yet a rich, cultural life. He told me today he wants to be a writer. Eventually.

SOPHIE. We should only live to see it.

MORRIS. [*He bends to kiss her and she turns her head away.*] What's the matter?

SOPHIE. You smell like a brewery. Where did you have dinner tonight?

MORRIS. Manny's Blue Room.

SOPHIE. And how many drinks did you have?

MORRIS. [*Taking off his jacket.*] Listen, what's with the questionnaire? If I want to relax a little, dinner time, have a couple of drinks, I got to have an accountant along, he should give you a certified statement?

SOPHIE. And who was the woman you were relaxing with, may I ask?

MORRIS. [*Rises.*] Which one of your private eyes sent you in a report? [*Picks up slippers from chair L.*] You're waiting here like a district attorney, I should put my foot in. [*Crosses to chair R. of bed and sits.*]

SOPHIE. It happens the Roselles were in the Blue Room tonight.

MORRIS. [*As he removes his shoes and puts on his slippers.*] Oh, so she's got to sit there, Mrs. Busybody Roselle, like a Russian spy, and run afterwards to call you. Who was the woman I was out with? Why didn't she come over in the restaurant and ask *me?*

SOPHIE. I suppose she was embarrassed.

MORRIS. Mrs. Roselle embarrassed! A barracuda is shy. Listen, I was in the Blue Room with Miss Menken, my designer, and I don't want to hear another word on this subject.

SOPHIE. Your designer?

MORRIS. I'm running a shop, I got to get out a line. If my designer's got problems, I got to listen.

SOPHIE. What kind of problems, for instance?

MORRIS. [*Rises, sits at R. side of bed.*] The worst kind. How would you like it, Sophie, to be a woman thirty-two, three—every night you come into an apartment house, good evening to the doorman, good evening to the elevator boy, you open the door to your flat and there's nobody there, except a cat, to say hello?

SOPHIE. You're only projecting. Maybe she prefers to live alone.

MORRIS. All I know is I got a temperamental designer. I don't want she should blow up in the middle of everything, quit and leave me without a line to open the season.

SOPHIE. Why are you raising your voice?

MORRIS. [*Crossing to chair L. puts his shoes down.*]
I am not raising it. I am *projecting* it. For God's sake,
can we stop this discussion already? [*Heatedly, as he
rips off his tie.*] I got to come home and have arguments with you, suspicions, one of your pals called you
to make a little trouble.

SOPHIE. Stop yelling. Jenny doesn't have to hear.

MORRIS. [*Removing his jacket.*] Never mind Jenny.
You're only worried I'll give your daughter a complex.
It's time somebody should worry about *my* complexes
in this house.

SOPHIE. Thank you very much.

MORRIS. [*Crossing toward the bathroom door.*]
Twenty-five years I've been checking in with you, like
a night watchman—[*Removing his tie.*]

SOPHIE. Very flattering for a wife to hear.

MORRIS. A wife hears what she deserves to hear. [*Takes
robe which is hanging on screen.*] She's got a few obligations too, you know. [*Crosses back ta* SOPHIE.]
I'm giving you fair warning, Sophie. Next time I come
home and find you with the cold cream on your face
and those irons in your head, you wouldn't have with
me an argument. I'll turn right around and go to the
club.

SOPHIE. What club?

MORRIS. So I'll *join* a club!

[*He strides to the bathroom, D.L.* SOPHIE *tries to control her laughter as we:*]

FADE OUT

ACT TWO

Scene III

Scene: *Next day. The showroom.*

At Rise: *The curtain is drawn back from Mr. Karp's pressing unit so that it may be seen Upstage.* KARP *himself is eating a hard-boiled egg which he has taken from an open lunch-box beside his pressing machine.* HAROLD *is in* MORRIS'S *office checking numbers and making notations on an inventory sheet. He has a slight bruise over one eye, possibly a small piece of adhesive to make it noticeable.*
The office door to the showroom is open.

KARP. [*From pressing machine.*] What is it with you young people today? You all got the world on your shoulders—

HAROLD. [*Moving into showroom.*] We've got it in our hair, Mr. Karp. You people dropped it—like Humpty Dumpty. I don't mean you, personally. Your generation.

KARP. [*Coming down to C.*] Listen, I heard this complaint already. My son came home from Korea, for two years he was mad on me, like I started the whole thing. I was standing here the whole time at the pressing machine. We had problems too, our generation. Maybe bigger problems than you. Couldn't walk on the street,

52

somebody would holler sheeny. Throw rocks on us. To make a living . . . And seems to me we didn't go around with such long faces all the time, blaming the older generation . . . You want an egg?

HAROLD. No, thanks.

KARP. Listen, don't be so worried. You're a young man. In the end, everything presses itself out. [*He crosses to chair U.L. and sits.*]

HAROLD. Ask your son about the refugees in Korea fighting on the road for scraps that fell from the garbage trucks. Ask him about the millions over there who go to bed hungry and hopeless while we spend billions for stuff to rot in granaries. How they'd feel waiting a couple of thousand years while everything presses itself out.

KARP. [*Defensively.*] Listen, all I said—[*As he speaks he rises and goes to pressing machine where he pours some coffee from a thermos into a cup and returns to his chair.*]

HAROLD. [*At table against R. wall.*] I know. I'm not sore at you, Mr. Karp. I'm a little wrought up just now about a certain landlord of my acquaintance.

KARP. You got something against landlords? Don't forget, I am a landlord too. Sixteen units in Jackson Heights.

HAROLD. Then you tell me—would you squeeze five grown people into a one bedroom flat?

KARP. Not if I would know. But you would be surprised how the tenants are staying up nights to put one over on the landlord.

HAROLD. Yeah. Well, that's a big help.

KARP. [*Plaintively.*] Listen, I worked plenty hard at this pressing machine, a good many years, to pay off the mortgages. You got it against me I want to have a little something now out of being a landlord?

[*As he talks,* KARP *has been repacking his lunchbox. On this last,* ROSENZWEIG *enters from R. 3 to C. He holds aloft a dress.*]

ROSENZWEIG. Again with the autobiography, Nathan? [*Brandishes the dress, shouting.*] This is a finished garment you sent me? What do you call this?

KARP. [*Hands over ears.*] Please, Rosie, you are busting my ear drums.

ROSENZWEIG. Look a seam a man presses. Twenty-five years at the machine. A senior member of the Union. An honorary pallbearer.

KARP. [*Rises, placating.*] All right. Give me the dress. [*Takes the dress from* ROSENZWEIG, *goes to his machine and starts to press.*] I'll press out the seam again. No tragedy.

ROSENZWEIG. And this time do it right! I got orders to get out! [*Starts to exit L.*]

HAROLD. [*Crossing in to* KARP.] You just going to stand there, let him holler at you like this?

[ROSENZWEIG *stops to listen.*]

KARP. [*Working the machine.*] Do I let him? He hollers.

HAROLD. Nobody's got a right to scream at you like that.

ROSENZWEIG. [*Turning in.*] Who asked you to butt in?

HAROLD. Look, Mr. Rosenzweig, don't start yelling at *me* now. I won't stand for it.

ROSENZWEIG. So don't stand for it. I run a shop here, not a kindergarten. [*Exits D.L.*]

HAROLD. Mr. Karp, don't press that dress. Not until he comes up and tells you, reasonably, what's wrong.

KARP. Listen, I don't want to make a federal case. A seam is crooked, I'll press it out again.

[HAROLD *takes hold of* KARP'S *arm and pulls him away from the machine.*]

HAROLD. Mr. Karp, you've worked hard all your life, you've earned the right to be treated like a human being, with a little dignity—

KARP. Harold, please. I worked here a good many years without dignity, I got an apartment house, three children, older than you, five grandchildren, God bless them, they don't want from me dignity either, only Cracker-jack and roller skates—do me a favor, leave me in peace to press out a dress.

LARRY. [*Enters L. 1, crosses to R.C.*] Hey, Harold, give me a hand. I got Magnuson of the Emporium outside, I want to show him a few samples.

[*At* LARRY'S *direction,* HAROLD *helps reposition show-room furnishings, then follows him out R. 3.* KARP *turns back to his machine—sees smoke rising from it. He grabs the dress that he's been working on, holds it up. It's scorched. He turns a stricken glance in the direction that* LARRY *and* HAROLD *have taken.*]

KARP. [*Shrieks.*]Rosie! [*Rushes out L. 1.*]

[LARRY *re-enters R. 3, pulls drapes U.L. to mask pressing machine, then crosses to L. 1 and ushers* MAGNUSON *and* MISS KELLY *into showroom.*]

LARRY. [*R. of* MAGNUSON.] Now look, Magnuson, I'm taking it on myself to show you these dresses, because I value your account and also your opinion—but if you flip over them, you've got to promise it won't be all over Seventh Ave. tomorrow morning that I gave you a preview of the line.

MAGNUSON. First wait until I flip—then you'll tell me I shouldn't shout it all over town. [*Sits in chair U.L.*]

LARRY. [*Calling.*] Okay, girls. Shelley.

SHELLEY. [*Entering from R. 3.*] Seven-thirty-eight.

[*Crosses D.C., circles to L., then U.R. and off R. 3.*]

LARRY. Heavy gold satin, pure silk—

MISS KELLEY. That's the harem poof skirt—

MAGNUSON. A striking creation. Would look wonderful in the windows. But who would buy it?

LARRY. Don't worry, you can sell this dress, Magnuson. Don't be afraid of this line.

MAGNUSON. What's the price of this dress?

LARRY. Haven't got the figures yet from Mr. Seidman. [*Calls.*] Tina.

TINA. [*Entering from L. 2.*] Seven-ninety-two. [*Crosses D.C., circles R., then U.C.*]

LARRY. Quilted orange, black and gold brocade—

MAGNUSON. What's with the ball gowns this season. I got customers never went to a ball in their life.

[TINA *exits L. 2.*]

LARRY. Well, this is the season to introduce them to a new way of life. [*Calls.*] Doreen.

DOREEN. [*Entering from L. 2.*] Seven-twenty-two.

MAGNUSON. Mm. Not bad.

MISS KELLEY. I like that back—especially with the train.

MAGNUSON. Make a note, Miss Kelley. Maybe a couple for the windows. [*To* LARRY.] Available in all shades?

LARRY. Here's the color range. [*Gets color chart from upstage table, then calls*] Edmae! [EDMAE *enters R. 3., crosses D.C., circles L., then up and off R. 3.*] This is Number Six-eight-four—isn't it lovely?

MISS KELLEY. I like it, it's very smart.

LARRY. Same color range. [*Calls.*] Shelley. [*Takes color chart from* MAGNUSON. *Replaces it on table Upstage.*]

SHELLEY. [*Entering from R. 3.*] Seven-eight-eight.

[*Crosses D.C., circles L., then starts up, as* MISS KELLEY *stops her.*]

LARRY. Red raw silk, two piece for evening—

MISS KELLEY. [*Writing.*] One minute, please, Straight skirt, overblouse, three quarter length-sleeves—

LARRY. Yes. The overblouse is beaded in black jet. [SHELLEY *exits R. 3.* LARRY *calls.*] Tina.

TINA. [*Entering from L. 2.*] Seven-oh-one. [*Comes D.C., circles, then up and off L. 2.*]

LARRY. Checked wool suit.

MAGNUSON. A two-piece number?

LARRY. Yes. And it comes with this cowl scarf, too. All French wool. [*Calls.*] Doreen.

DOREEN. [*Entering from L. 2.*] Six-twenty-five. [*She models the dress then drifts Upstage.*]

MISS KELLEY. I think this number should be wonderful for us, Mr. Magnuson.

LARRY. We call it Etruscan Modern.

MAGNUSON. [*To* LARRY.] For a simple dress, its a little extreme, no?

[HAROLD *wanders in from R. 3.*]

LARRY. You mean it's got a little class. What do you want—bustles? [*Observing* HAROLD.] Meet the boss's son, Harold. Mr. Magnuson of the Emporium in Little Rock. That's a name you'll hear about.

HAROLD. [*Crosses to* MAGNUSON *and shakes hands.*] I've heard of Little Rock.

LARRY. [*Quickly pulling* HAROLD *away.*] Finest department store in the South. His buyer, Miss Kelley. Harold's coming into the business. Part of our forward looking policy. Training young executives for the future.

MAGNUSON. Stop. You're trying to make like General Motors? [*To* HAROLD, *with a sardonic edge.*] What do you think, young man? Arkansas is not New York. Could I sell a garment like this to my customers?

HAROLD. What color?

LARRY. [*Brings down* DOREEN *to distract* MAGNUSON. *Again to the rescue and with a baleful glance at* HAROLD.] All colors. This number'll go in all colors-- high shades as well as staple—we're going to use a lot of pottery colors this season—

MAGNUSON. All right. Put me down for a run of sizes, all colors.

[DOREEN *exits L. 2.*]

LARRY. [*Relieved at the narrow escape.*] Are you kidding? I'm not even supposed to be showing you these styles. I'll take your order, delivery date unspecified— after our Style Show. [*Gets order book from table Upstage.*]

MAGNUSON. You mean I got to leave it to you, color, sizes, delivery, everything?

LARRY. If you want to order now. Or you can wait until the Style Show and stand in line.

MISS KELLEY. [*To* HAROLD.] How would this make up in peau do soie, Mr. Seidman?

HAROLD. [*Hesitates a moment.*] I've been in the dress business about four hours. I don't know peau de soie from burlap. [MISS KELLEY *laughs. A wintry smile crosses* MAGNUSON's *face.*] I know this much. You could close your eyes and order anything my father'll send you.

MAGNUSON. For open orders I don't need buyers, I don't need jet service, I could stay home and order by mail.

LARRY. [*With a diplomatic smile.*] Harold--Mr. Magnuson's rated one of the smartest buyers of merchandise in this country—

MAGNUSON. No, let the boy talk. Your father's such a genius, he sent me a shipment three years ago—

LARRY. [*Crossing above* MAGNUSON.] Ah, come on, Magnuson. Don't rake that up.

MAGNUSON. Every shwarze in Little Rock was wearing the same dress.

HAROLD. [*Instantly bridling.*] Do you object to colored people appreciating good style too?

MAGNUSON. What I object to, young man, is for my customers to pay me a hundred and thirty-nine-fifty for a dress and then meet themselves coming and going, with every hired girl, in the same dress at nineteen-seventy-five.

HAROLD. Well, that's quite a problem, Mr. Magnuson. Maybe we ought to get the colored people down south back into loin clothes and crocodile teeth.

[MAGNUSON *flashes a look at* LARRY *who moves toward* HAROLD *to head off disaster.*]

LARRY. Come on, Harold. Quit kidding around. Mr. Magnuson is taking you seriously. Tell him you were kidding.

HAROLD. Yeah—E pluribus unum. I was just kidding, Mr. Magnuson.

MAGNUSON. [*Magnanimously.*] Well, I could take a little kidding, with the next man.

LARRY. [*Calling.*] Shelley.

[SHELLEY *enters R. 3, comes down, shows back to audience.*]

SHELLEY. Number seven-sixteen.

LARRY. Isn't that a beautiful tweed? Notice that front panel. Smart, huh?

[SHELLEY *crosses up and exits R. 3.*]

MAGNUSON. Tell me, Mr. Seidman Junior, you're going on the road sometimes?

HAROLD. I imagine I will—when I've learned enough to know what I'm talking about.

MAGNUSON. [*Obviously approving this humility.*] You'll learn. You'll learn. I could see, you got a good head on your shoulders. Listen, you'll be down our way, I want you should stop in and see me. You got a standing invitation to my house for dinner. You're engaged, maybe?

HAROLD. No.

MAGNUSON. I want you to meet my daughter. She is a very fine piano player. [*Expansively, rising and crossing R. to HAROLD.*] A young man like you, with respect, willing to admit he don't know everything, to learn— you got a big future in this business.

HAROLD. [*Politely.*] Thank you. How large a store do you have, Mr. Magnuson?

MAGNUSON. [*Jovially, to LARRY.*] Right away he wants to know. [*To HAROLD.*] Big enough for a son-in-law.

Six floors, four hundred employees, lounge, patio, children's playroom—

HAROLD. What percentage of your employees are Negroes, Mr. Magnuson?

[EVERYBODY *freezes as if for a still.*]

MAGNUSON. [*Recovering from the shock.*] What is it—you're taking a census?

HAROLD. I was just wondering. You do employ them, don't you?

LARRY. [*Frantically, crossing down.*] Harold!

MAGNUSON. [*Turning balefully to* LARRY.] Listen, what is going on here? I got to pass a test to buy dresses here?

LARRY. [*Futilely.*] You know—young man—he hasn't got his feet wet yet.

MAGNUSON. But a big mouth he's certainly got.

LARRY. [*Calls off U.L.*] Tina! is Six-thirty-four ready yet? [TINA *enters L. 2, crosses D.C.*] This is our Six-thirty-four, and this is one number I want you to make a special note of.

HAROLD. [*With an edge.*] I just want to know how a prominent merchant in Little Rock deals with the Negro question.

MAGNUSON. I got a business to run. I pay taxes. Let the politicians break their heads with this question!

LARRY. [*Desperately.*] We expect this to be very big. You can really get volume on this one.

HAROLD. Don't *you* have to sleep nights? You're a Jew, Mr. Magnuson. Doesn't discrimination mean anything to you?

[LARRY *despairingly ushers* TINA *out L. 2.*]

MAGNUSON. [*Reddening with anger.*] Listen, you young snot, that bandage over your eye—maybe you got it asking questions are none of your goddam business?

HAROLD. [*Reacting with anger.*] Suppose I ask you if your talented daughter plays piano only on the white keys. Or does she sometimes bring herself to use the black?

MAGNUSON. [*Rises, furious.*] I wish I was your father five minutes. I would give you black. Black and blue. [*To* MISS KELLEY, *as he starts out.*] Come on, Miss Kelley.

[MISS KELLEY *exits L. 1.*]

LARRY. Magnuson, wait a minute—

MAGNUSON. For what? I got to stay and listen to this crap, I haven't got it coming out of my ears already from all the cockeye radicals back home?

[*He strides out, following* MISS KELLEY. LARRY *gives* HAROLD *a look that substitutes for a bookful of words.*]

LARRY. Magnuson—wait—

HAROLD. What's the matter? Are we that hard up for business?

LARRY. [*He shakes his head in impotent exasperation, then turns and hurries after the others.*] Magnuson— listen—[*Exits L. 1.*]

ROSENZWEIG. [*Entering from L. 2.*] Wait a minute, Mr. Junior Executive, what's all the yelling?

HAROLD. That's a good question coming from you, Mr. Rosenzweig.

ROSENZWEIG. Look, I just got one question to ask you—are you going back to college in the fall?

HAROLD. No, but—

ROSENSWEIG. That's all I want to know. [*Crosses into office through R. 2.* HAROLD *exits L. 2.*] Morris— [*He sees that Morris is not in his office and hits the intercom switch.*] Miss Weintraub, where is Mr.—?

MORRIS. [*Enters from office door, R. 1, goes to his desk; he is in shirt sleeves.*] What's the matter, Rosenzweig? Another calamity?

ROSENZWEIG. I got two words for you, Mr. Seidman. Get yourself another production man.

MORRIS. [*Sits back, looks at* ROSENZWEIG *with mingled amusement and exasperation.*] You're in so deep, give me already two more words and tell me why.

ROSENZWEIG. I don't want to have any arguments, debates—I'll just turn in my apron and let me go.

MORRIS. You can keep the apron. With my compliments. What's with you, Rosenzweig? What's going on?

ROSENZWEIG. I'm getting an apoplexy, that's what's going on. And it's from your son—

MORRIS. With a boy who's been in the shop a half day you got to have fights already?

ROSENZWEIG. Just let me quit. Please.

MORRIS. Tell me what happened? You got time to quit.

ROSENZWEIG. Just now I go in to talk to Karp about a sample—

LARRY. [*Enters L. 1, goes into office through R. 2.*] Well, there goes Magnuson.

MORRIS. What, Magnuson?

LARRY. He came in to take a look at the line and in the middle—

MORRIS. You showed him the line?

LARRY. Well, he's a big account, he was in town, I thought I'd make a little time with him, whet his appetite.

MORRIS. Larry, if we're going to show everybody the line, what do we need a Style Show—?

LARRY. Don't worry. Magnuson won't be there. Your son fixed that up.

ROSENZWEIG. I'm not surprised.

MORRIS. Rosenzweig, do me a favor. Go down to Manny's. Have a good lunch and charge it to me.

ROSENZWEIG. Lunch, he says. I got a fire in my stomach and he tells me lunch. [ROSENZWEIG *exits through showroom and off L. 1.*]

LARRY. What's with the boy, Morris? He seems to have it in for the whole world.

MORRIS. [*Crosses L.*] And if he has—it's such a fine, wonderful world?

LARRY. [*Crossing D.R. of* MORRIS.] Okay, but do we have to reform it in our showroom? Especially with a guy like Magnuson drooling over the line? You ought to have a talk with the kid, Morris.

MORRIS. [*Instantly defensive.*] I'll take care of Harold. [*Change of tone.*] Magnuson. He liked the line?

LARRY. I told you—he flipped over it.

MORRIS. So, Mr. Style Expert, what have you got to say about our fancy designer, now?

LARRY. The gal is tremendous. Like I always said.

MORRIS. Sure. Like you always said.

LARRY. [*Sits in chair below desk.*] I hear you tied one on at Manny's last night.

[MORRIS *looks at him, balanced between exasperation and his sense of the ridiculous.*]

MORRIS. [*Crossing to* LARRY.] Where did *you* get your report?

LARRY. A little bird told me.

MORRIS. [*Shaking his head.*] A little bird.

LARRY. I heard you and your—er—date put away so many drinks you had Leo dizzy, he couldn't count any more.

MORRIS. Don't worry. He counted. It was all on the bill.

[INTERCOM *buzzes.* MORRIS *answers.*]

MISS WEINTRAUB'S VOICE. Your sister is calling, Mr. Seidman. From Flushing.

MORRIS. I don't want to talk to her.

MISS WEINTRAUB'S VOICE. This is the third time she's called. She sounds kind of frantic.

MORRIS. This is a novelty? All right, put her on. [*Picks up phone.*] Yes. Bessie . . . Yes, I was late this morning. I stopped off in the bank to count my money . . . Who's in my office? Well, let's see, I got here a barber and a manicurist and a boy with a fan, he's keeping away the flies . . . [*Voice rising uncontrollably.*] What do you mean, me and my Cafe Society bums? Are you crazy? . . . Myron heard this? Where did Myron heard this? . . . I see. A little bird told him. This little bird is getting around on a bicycle. [LARRY *reacts.* MORRIS *sits down now at his desk.*]All right, you may as well know, Bessie. A man my age, I figure it's getting pretty close to the end, I want to have a fling or two before they put me away in the cemetery . . . Naturally, another woman. Who do you want me to have an affair with—another man? [*From L. 2* KARP *enters, to office door R. 2, woebegone. He takes in* MORRIS *on the phone and* LARRY; *withdraws.*] Listen, Bessie, better go back to your television, you are spoiling the whole Nielsen rating there in Flushing . . . Call up the Times, the District Attorney, all the relatives, don't bother me with your nonsense, I got a business to run and goodbye. [*He puts the phone down, emphatically.*]

LARRY. Looks like the news is getting around.

MORRIS. [*Suddenly confidential.*] Well, who cares? Like you said, Larry. Vanilla, vanilla. A person gets tired. He wants to try sometimes a little tutti-frutti. [LARRY, *flabbergasted, rises, closes door to showroom, turns to face* MORRIS.] What are you looking so stunned?

LARRY. You and the Menken dame—right in the same shop. You know what you're doing, Morris? It's dynamite.

MORRIS. I don't understand you, Larry. Isn't this the advice you gave me yesterday?

LARRY. [*Crossing D.L.*] You know damn well I was kidding. I've always respected you—what you stood for— [*Sits down on bench R.*]

MORRIS. I know. For me you got only the highest moral standards. [*Rises and crosses to* LARRY.] Tell the truth, Larry. You're worried for my reputation, or my family —or you're just plain jealous?

LARRY. Don't be ridiculous. You know how long it would take me to make this broad if I thought it was worth the trouble?

MORRIS. You're mistaken, Larry. [MISS MENKEN *enters showroom from L. 2 and knocks at other door R. 2.*] Yes?

MISS MENKEN. [*Pokes her head in.*] Have you a minute, both of you. [*She returns to showroom.*]

MORRIS. Certainly, Miss Menken. [*To* LARRY, *confidentially.*] Forget it, Larry. This is one number that won't go in your little black book. [*To* MISS MENKEN, *as he enters showroom.*] How are you, Miss Menken. How do you feel? How did you sleep?

[LARRY *enters showroom.*]

MISS MENKEN. [*Responding warmly to* MORRIS'S *query.*] Like a baby . . . I've been thinking about the collection. I thought we'd open— [*Crosses to L. 2 and calls.*] Doreen, will you come in, please.

[KARP *peeks in again, timidly, from L. 2, sees that* MORRIS IS ENGAGED *and withdraws as before.* DOREEN *enters L. 1, modeling a striking evening dress.*]

MORRIS. [*Crosses D.L. and sits.*] Beautiful. Beautiful. This came out very well. Like I said, you are an artist, Miss Menken.

LARRY. [*Goes to* DOREEN, *inspects the dress.*] Turn around, Doreen. [*To* MISS MENKEN.) This dress has got it, Miss Menken. Really got it. [*He crosses L. and stands above* MORRIS'S *chair.*]

MISS MENKEN. So glad you approve. [*To* MORRIS, *ignoring* LARRY.] I thought we'd open with seven-oh-seven the pimento evening gown, and use this one— [SHELLEY *has just entered from R. 3 wearing a beautiful, elaborate evening dress.*] Seven-eighteen, to close the Show.

MORRIS. Stunning. Stunning. I hope we can get the full color range from the textile people.

[BOTH GIRLS *parade Downstage, then Upstage.*]

MISS MENKEN. What I'd like to try for is a certain rhythm, both in color and design—a kind of crescendo of feeling.

LARRY. I've got it right now. Now we're talking.

MISS MENKEN. [*Indicating* SHELLEY'S DRESS.] On this one, I thought we could have a matching stole.

MORRIS. Perfect. Perfect.

MISS MENKEN. Thank you, girls. [DOREEN *and* SHELLEY *exit R. 3.*] Now, if Mr. Rosenzweig doesn't develop a brand new ulcer—it'll take a little more material than we figured in the pattern—

MORRIS. [*Rises, crosses to* MISS MENKEN.] I'll lay out the pattern myself, I'll find you the yardage. It's not a big talent, like Beethoven's, but I got a knack for it. [*He leads her Upstage.* KARP *again pokes his woebegone face in at the door.*] Nathan, stop already playing peek-a-boo. You want to come in, come in.

KARP. You're not too busy?

MISS MENKEN. I'm just leaving, Mr. Karp.

MORRIS. [*To* MISS MENKEN.] Have a good lunch, dear. I couldn't be happier about these garments. [*She gives him a warm smile as she exits R. 3.*]

LARRY. Dear! [*Disgusted, he exits L. I.* MORRIS *turns to* KARP, *brings him Downstage.*]

MORRIS. So, Nathan. What's on your mind? What are you looking so worried? You lost a tenant? [*Sits in chair, R.*]

KARP. [*At C. Tragically.*] I burned a dress.

MORRIS. You burned a dress? What dress?

KARP. Seven-twenty-two. The sample.

MORRIS. [*Rises, concerned.*] How did it happen? You're tired, sick, what?

KARP. You wouldn't like it. I got to tell you. It's Harold. He makes me so nervous—

MORRIS. [*Bridling instantly.*] How does he make you so nervous?

KARP. I don't know. Questions. Questions.

MORRIS. And you're such a sourpuss you can't stand it a boy asks questions? What kind of questions?

KARP. Do I know? Dignity, Refugees, Humpty-Dumpty—

MORRIS. I don't know what the hell you are talking about. If *you* know, and you got a complaint [*Crossing D.L.*] take it up with the Grievance Committee. I got enough on my head.

KARP. Please. *Don't holler!*

MORRIS. What's the matter you become so sensitive all of a sudden? Twenty years Rosenzweig is hollering on you, it's all right. Me, the boss, I can't raise my voice.

KARP. Yes. Rosenzweig I don't care. But since when are you with me a boss?

MORRIS. [*Crossing to* KARP.] Nathan, what do you want from my life? You burned a dress. A sample. You want I should apologize to you?

KARP. I want you should tell your son—

MORRIS. [*Crossing to office door.*] Don't tell me what I should tell my son. Somebody else burns a dress I would dock his pay or fire him. [*Crossing back to* KARP, *angrily.*] With you, it becomes a family argument.

KARP. You want to dock me? Go ahead. Maybe I should quit altogether.

MORRIS. All right. You want to quit, quit. [*He goes into his office—sits down at his desk.*]

KARP. [*Enters office.*] Quit. Quit. Twenty years I been working for you, you never told me before to quit.

MORRIS. So maybe it's time you should learn. I'm your employer, and I want from you a little respect. Plain talk.

KARP. Plain talk. Respect. On Bleecker Street, you needed somebody to stay till two, three o'clock in the morning, you didn't want from me respect. Eight months I didn't draw from you a cent salary, I lent you yet money for lunch, you didn't want from me respect. All right. Call up the accounting department. Take off for the dress I burned. And don't cheat yourself. [*He starts for door, breaks down and cries. Overcome with contrition,* MORRIS *goes to him.*]

MORRIS. Nathan, wait. I'm sorry. I didn't mean anything. You know what a temper I got. You think I care about a burned dress? You could burn fifty dresses. Listen, come, sit down. I'll send down for some coffee—

KARP. No. I'm ashamed. Let me alone.

MORRIS. Please, Nathan. Don't make me feel like a criminal. Nathan—[*Uncertainly.*] You're going back to the machine?

KARP. [*Turns to him now.*] Where else should I go? To the Peppermint Lounge? [*He goes out.* MORRIS *stands looking after him for a moment, then with an air of decision, goes to his desk and switches on the* INTERCOM.]

MORRIS. Miss Weintraub, send in my son.

MISS WEINTRAUB'S VOICE. He went out, Mr. Seidman.

MORRIS. Out?

MISS WEINTRAUB'S VOICE. He didn't say. I suppose lunch.

MORRIS. [*Raised voice.*] Lunch. It's nearly three o'clock.

MISS WEINTRAUB'S VOICE. Please, Mr. Seidman! This is an amplifier.

MORRIS. I'm sorry, Miss Weintraub. I'm a little upset today. Let me know, please, when he gets back.

MISS WEINTRAUB'S VOICE. There's a young lady waiting for him, too.

MORRIS. Here in the shop? Who is she?

MISS WEINTRAUB'S VOICE. A Miss Sowolska.

MORRIS. [*Tensing.*] Send her in. [*He enters showroom and waits.* HELEN SOWALSKA *enters showroom from L. 1. She is dressed in beatnik style, with thong sandals and pants.* MORRIS *looks expressively at her outfit while she looks timidly at him.*]

HELEN. How do you do, Mr. Seidman?

MORRIS. [*Loins girded.*] Listen, Miss Sowalska, I don't know what you got in mind visiting my son here, but this is a place of business, and my son is an employee like anybody else. He is not receiving visitors during working hours. Good day. [*Starts for his office.*]

HELEN. [*Tremulously.*] I know, I'm sorry if I make a nuisance, but I must tell Harold about the landlord—

MORRIS. What about the landlord?

HELEN. [*Increasingly shaky.*] There is trouble. The landlord has made a complaint.

MORRIS. I thought it was Harold got out the complaint.

HELEN. Yes, to the Health Department, but now it is the police. For battering and assault. Harold had a fight with the landlord last night.

MORRIS. [*Claps a hand to his head, then rushes into his office and hits the* INTERCOM *switch.* HELEN *follows him in.*] Miss Weintraub, get me my lawyer, right away. [HELEN *is controlling her emotion with an effort.* MORRIS *stands above her now.*] Miss Sowalska, give me an idea, rationally, what is going on—

HELEN. Someone came from the Health Department to make a report and when the landlord found out, he was very angry and he came over with a notice that we must move because we are behind in the rent. My father got into a fight with the landlord. Harold was there and he made the landlord a bloody nose.

MORRIS. He made the landlord a bloody nose?

HELEN. And this morning a policeman came looking for them and took my father to the station house.

MORRIS. [*Crosses to his desk.*] This boy is a genius. What he could accomplish in one day—

HELEN. [*Tearfully, crossing to* MORRIS.] Mr. Seidman, I am so frightened. To be mixed up with police and courts—we are not citizens and if we get in trouble with the immigration, they will send us back—

MORRIS. [*Gives her his handkerchief.*] They wouldn't send you back. [*He ushers her to chair R. below desk.*] It's not Poland here with the courts and police.

[BUZZER *sounds.*]

MISS WEINTRAUB'S VOICE. I have Mr. Handelsman for you.

MORRIS. Put him on. And send Mr. Karp in here. [*Picks up phone.*] Hello, Saul. Listen. I got a lot of business for you today. . . . No, not collections . . . assault and battery. Harold hit somebody. . . . A landlord. . . . Sure, it could be worse, could have been a policeman. . . . Saul, take care of it. . . . And I want you to bail me out somebody, . . . a Mr. Sowalska. [*To the* GIRL.] What is the station house where they took him?

HELEN. Mott Street.

MORRIS. [*Into phone.*] The Mott Street station house. . . . Yes, get him out, whatever it is . . . [KARP *enters from L. 2, through showroom to office.*] All right, I'll explain you the whole thing later. Goodbye. [*Puts phone down.*] Nathan, you got a apartment for rent, big enough for five people?

KARP. How big are the people?

MORRIS. [*Impatiently.*] They're *people.*

KARP. [*Dubiously.*] Happens I got an apartment, on the ground floor, the tenants just moved out. There's small children?

HELEN. Seven and ten.

KARP. [*Calamitously.*] The worst age—crayolas on the walls, roller skating in the hall, bicycles—

HELEN. Oh, no! Anton and Eva are very quiet. They do not skate—

KARP. I got to get more on the rent—

MORRIS. All right, Nathan. The name is Sowalska. Get the place ready. I'll guarantee the rent. [KARP *exits through showroom and off L. 2.*]

HELEN. Mr. Seidman, how will we pay you back?

MORRIS. Don't worry, I wouldn't sue you.

HELEN. I was so frightened. [*She starts to cry from sheer relief.*]

MORRIS. Come on, stop already with the faucet. [*She looks up at him gratefully as* HAROLD *enters D.L., crosses and enters office through R. 1.*]

HAROLD. [*At L.C.*] Hey, what's going on here? Helen. What are you doing here? [*She rushes to him.*]

[INTERCOM buzzes.]

MORRIS. Yes.

MISS WEINTRAUB'S VOICE. Mr. Seidman, your son just got back. [MORRIS *reacts, with a quizzical look at* HAROLD.]

HELEN. [*Tearfully, gladly.*] It is all right now. Your father has arranged everything—about the landlord—

[MORRIS *crosses below desk.*]

HAROLD. Is that so? [*Turning, crosses to* MORRIS.] Look Pa, how about letting me take care of my own problems?

MORRIS. Sure. I'll let you take care—you'll be in jail with Mr. Sowalska, and his family will be on the street—

HAROLD. It happens Mr. Sowalska's home right now—

HELEN. He is home?

HAROLD. I just left him there.

MORRIS. I thought he was in the station house.

HAROLD. I put up some bail—

MORRIS. How? With what?

HAROLD. What's the difference? I put up the registration on my car as security for bond.

MORRIS. And what's with the assault and battery?

HAROLD. I'll handle that when it comes up.

MORRIS. It's up. I told my lawyer to get in touch with the landlord—

HAROLD. [*Strongly.*] Pa, if I need a lawyer, I'll *get* one. If I have to pay a fine, I'll pay it. If I have to sit in jail, okay. And I'll gladly do *double* the time for another crack at that greedy face!

HELEN. [*Crosses to* HAROLD.] Harold, you should not speak so to your father.

HAROLD. Look, go home, will you? I'll see you later.

HELEN. I do not understand. Why are you so angry—?

HAROLD. [*Takes her arm, starts her toward door.*] Helen—please—

HELEN. All right, Harold.

MORRIS. Go, Miss Sowalska. Everything will be all right. I promise you. [*She turns back, kisses him impulsively, then turns to* HAROLD *who gives her a perfunctory embrace. She leaves through showroom and off D.L.* MORRIS *sits down at his desk.* HAROLD *turns to his* FATHER.] She's a lovely girl, Harold.

HAROLD. [*Crosses D.L.*] Thank you. Well, you've had a grand time, haven't you—playing the big shot with Helen.

MORRIS. Are you crazy? This is all I got to do. I had some day from you today. A regular parade of your fans.

HAROLD. You want me to quit, Pa?

MORRIS. [*Rises, crosses Downstage.*] Quit? You haven't even started yet! One day you're in the shop, Magnuson, Rosenzweig wants to quit—Karp—

HAROLD. Just because I can't stand the way Rosenzweig hollers at him!

MORRIS. This is his nature. A canary sings; Rosenzweig hollers.

HAROLD. Well, my nature is to react when somebody is treated like dirt. And this Magnuson, too. Imagine. Down there in Little Rock—a Jew—

MORRIS. Harold, if I had to do business only with people whose private lives and politics I like, I could close my doors tomorrow.

HAROLD. Okay, I'll put on a muzzle from now on. This is a place of business, God's in his heaven, and the customer is always right. Okay, can I go now? [*Crossing up toward door.*]

MORRIS. No, you can't go now. I want you to take a lesson from what happened today. It's not a business for amateurs, helping people. With too much heart and no judgment you could make as much of a mish-mash in the world as with no heart at all. You want to help people? Make something of yourself first. Have a position, influence—and money doesn't hurt either. Then you could help. Not sit around talking about truth all night and in the morning jump up and punch a landlord in the nose—

HAROLD. [*Losing control, crossing down.*] Why did you have to mix in? Why did you have to go behind my back, make me look like a fool in front of Helen, wet behind the ears—?

MORRIS. [*Crosses L.*] Harold, I know we don't speak the same language any more—

HAROLD. Damn it! Can't I make you understand? I want you and Ma to stop interfering in my private life—

MORRIS. Private life. I wonder what's been happening with your life altogether. I used to be very proud of you. Where did you learn to open up such a mouth? From those philosophers in the coffee house?

HAROLD. [*Stung; bitterly.*] What's so great about *your* life, Pa? That you can order around a hundred people in the shop here, and five dollar steaks? Is that what puts you up there, making pronouncements? Maybe

those friends of mine you despise wouldn't trade places
with you for anything in the world. [MORRIS *sinks down
on bench L.*] Making such a thing about how you
struggled—what did you struggle for? A vault full of
stocks and bonds? Is that the Holy Grail or something?
Maybe they don't think you're such a howling success.
Maybe they think you're a *miserable failure,* all of you
who turned this country—[MORRIS *rises impulsively,
slaps his face, hard. For a moment or two they stare
at each other, stunned by the sudden utterly unfamiliar
act of violence.*] Okay, Pa. You've won the argument.
I'm convinced.

[*He goes out, closing office door behind him, and exits
U.L.* MORRIS *sits as if stunned.* INTERCOM *buzzes once
and then again.* MORRIS *rises wearily, goes to his desk
and flips the switch.*]

MISS WEINTRAUB'S VOICE. A Mr. Gurewitz from the
Bialystocker Lodge to see you.

MORRIS. What does he want?

MISS WEINTRAUB'S VOICE. It's about cemetery plots.

MORRIS. Tell him I don't need one. I'm fitted already.
[*He sits for a moment, then on an impulse he flips the
intercom switch.*] Miss Weintraub—

MISS WEINTRAUB'S VOICE. Yes?

MORRIS. Would you ask Miss Menken to come in,
please. I would like to—talk to her.

MISS WEINTRAUB'S VOICE. She went out, Mr. Seidman.

MORRIS. Out?

MISS WEINTRAUB'S VOICE. Yes, she went over to Manny's Blue Room with Larry Kogen.

MORRIS. Oh— [*He shuts off the switch, feeling sunk.*]

[WILENSKI *enters the showroom, L. 1, crosses and looks into Morris' office.*]

WILENSKI. Hello, Seidman. You're busy?

MORRIS. Again, Wilenski?

WILENSKI. [*Coming in.*] What again? I was just in the building—having a session with your competitor upstairs. [*Mopping his brow, crosses to chair below desk and sits.*] You think you're a tough man? Compared to this monster you're a regular Santa Claus. [*He sits down—senses* MORRIS' *dejection.*] What's the matter, Seidman? You look depressed.

MORRIS. [*Sighs heavily.*] Small children, small troubles —big children, big troubles.

WILENSKI. What happened?

MORRIS. Nothing. My son just told me I was a failure.

WILENSKI. Failure! The nerve of the kids these days. My son would say something like that to me, I would give him such a clop in the face—!

MORRIS. [*Eyeing him sorrowfully.*] You would, ha? And this, you think, is the action of a responsible parent?

WILENSKI. A parent isn't human? It's not so bad to give a boy a slap once in a while. My analyst told me a parent's got a perfect right to react, also. He's not just a slot machine for giving out bicycles and bar mitzvah suits.

MORRIS. What—you're back with the analyst?

WILENSKI. Yeah, for a couple months already.

MORRIS. I thought he gave you a diploma.

WILENSKI. I need a couple booster shots. You know, men our age—problems. With the children—the home life—sex—

MORRIS. Sex? Listen, men our age, we're lucky if it's still a problem.

WILENSKI. You'd be surprised. Makes sense what he says, the analyst. You start to dig down into yourself deep—at the end of every tunnel, what do you find? Sex.

MORRIS. [*Rising, crosses to bench L. and sits.*] Some big secret he found out from Mr. Freud.

WILENSKI. Freud is by you a nothing? Look, maybe it wouldn't be such a bad idea for you to have a few sessions with the analyst.

MORRIS. What does he charge?

WILENSKI. Seidman, what's the difference? You're a rich man—

MORRIS. Tell me, did you ever discuss with your analyst why you are always counting my money?

WILENSKI. All right. Thirty-five dollars an hour.

MORRIS. [*Aghast, rises.*] Thirty-five—?

WILENSKI. Send for a plumber, you'll pay twelve.

MORRIS. [*Crosses to his desk and sits.*] I can get this same advice from Larry for nothing. And my sister Bessie throws in yet a glass tea.

WILENSKI. [*Rising, crosses to bench L. and sits.*] Think it over. I promise you it's the best investment you'll ever make.

MORRIS. So why are *you* back on the couch?

WILENSKI. We don't know yet. I got this stiff neck. And a couple months ago I started having those dreams again. About falling off a cliff.

MORRIS. It's the same cliff—in Fallsburg?

WILENSKI. I don't know. A cliff. Only now it's not me who's falling off. It's my wife.

MORRIS. You're sure you're not giving her a little push?

WILENSKI. [*Dismisses the whole subject with a wave of his hand and a sigh.*] No, it's much more complicated. Aah, let the analyst break *his* head. [*Rising.*] Listen, how's about coming with me to the Turkish Bath? I got a new masseur there, a regular Samson—he'll crack your bones, you'll feel like a new man.

MORRIS. No, thanks. I don't have time. [*Rising.*] But I tell you—I'll go down to Manny's with you for a drink. [*Flips the* INTERCOM.] Miss Weintraub, I'm going out with Mr. Wilenski. I'll be back soon. [*Shuts off the switch, takes his jacket, as before off the dummy and puts it on. Both go out into showroom.*]

WILENSKI. Drink? What kind of a drink?

MORRIS. It's called a vodka gimlet.

WILENSKI. A vodka gimlet?

MORRIS. You got to try it, Wilenski. I promise you—three of them and you'll be dreaming your *analyst* is falling off the cliff.

FADEOUT

ACT TWO

Scene IV

SCENE: *The showroom. Re-position Upstage
table to C.*

AT RISE: MISS MENKEN *enters from L. 1,
striding briskly.* LARRY *follows, a few steps
behind.*

LARRY. [*As both stop at table, C.*] Hey, slow down.
You must've been on the track team at Bryn Mawr.

MISS MENKEN. [*Goes into* MORRIS'S *office through
R. 2.*] I've really got some work to do, Mr. Kogen.

LARRY. [*Following her to office door.*] Come on. You've
knocked out a couple dozen gorgeous numbers in a
matter of weeks. You're entitled to relax a bit—

MISS MENKEN. [*Brushing past him back to showroom.*]
You're in a remarkably pleasant mood today. Must be
something you ate.

LARRY. Yes—a lot of crow. But you won't give me a
chance. [*Shaking his head.*] Man—you Bryn Mawr
girls—to get through the barbed wire.

[*As he speaks,* MISS MENKEN *removes her coat,* LARRY
hangs it up on a dress rack.]

MISS MENKEN. [*Relenting a bit.*] I'm sorry, Mr. Kogen.
I was just getting even. You *have* given me a pretty
bad time, you know.

LARRY. [*Brightening.*] That's better—much better. Why, in a year or two you might even call me Larry.

[*She gives him an amused glance, starts to check dresses on the rack against figures in an inventory book she takes up from table.*]

MISS MENKEN. What *is* your real name—Lawrence?

LARRY. No—Isadore. [*They both laugh. The ice between them is beginning to thaw.*] Hey, you would have gotten a charge out of the way old Magnuson went for Six-twenty-five. He didn't even blink when I said Etruscan Modern.

MISS MENKEN. Did you offer to throw in a set of dishes?

LARRY. [*Laughs.*] Listen, that cookie knows style. [*Then.*] This Etruscan stuff, you must've picked that up in Italy. You spent a couple of years there, didn't you?

MISS MENKEN. [*Removes a dress from rack.*] Why this sudden interest in my career?

LARRY. Well—could be it's not really sudden.

MISS MENKEN. [*Appears to be absorbed in examining the dress.*] Now Mr. Kogen, you musn't turn your legendary charm on me full blast like this. It's overpowering.

LARRY. Fine chance. What's this legendary bit. You been getting an earful from Doreen?

MISS MENKEN. [*Returns dress to rack.*] No, as a matter of fact, it was Mr. Seidman. He said that hard-bitten buyers and models turned tremulous as brides before your boyish grin.

LARRY. How come I got into the conversation last night, anyway?

MISS MENKEN. Oh, you just popped up—[*Deadpan, making an entry in a notebook.*] I don't recall the exact connection, but I said I thought you were about forty-five—

LARRY. Forty-five! You kidding? I don't look any forty-five. [*Concerned.*] No kidding. Do I look forty-five? [*As he catches her expression.*] Aha, the needle again.

MISS MENKEN. [*Smiling.*] Just a conditioned reflex, I guess.

LARRY. Well, you started it—giving me that use-the-back-entrance feeling.

MISS MENKEN. Funny, I thought I was defending myself.

LARRY. So it's a standoff. Bryn Mawr meets the slot-machine set half way. How about it? [*He holds out his hand; she takes it. He holds onto it until she draws it away.*] So we've got an armistice to celebrate. How about dinner tonight?

MISS MENKEN. [*Uncertainly.*] Mm—I don't know—

LARRY. Got another date—with the boss?

MISS MENKEN. [*Bridling.*] Mr. Kogen, it wasn't a date—

LARRY. [*Quickly.*] Okay—Okay—. Why don't we drive out to the Island for a shore dinner this evening? You like sea food?

MISS MENKEN. Love it.

LARRY. I know a great place down there. Just the owner and a dozen tables. But they've got stone crab—and they make a red snapper soup—you've got to taste it to believe it.

MISS MENKEN. Sounds marvelous.

LARRY. Great. Why don't you knock off around four? I'll pick you up at your place around five. Maybe you'll throw some things in a bag—shorts, bathing suit— after dinner we'll drive out somewhere—

MISS MENKEN. Drive out somewhere?

LARRY. Yeah. Along the shore. Southampton—I know a great beach—

MISS MENKEN. MIAMI Beach?

LARRY. You want to? I'm game. We could make it a long weekend.

MISS MENKEN. Doesn't take you long to get down to cases, does it?

LARRY. Look, we're both over twenty-one. What do you say? There's a plane leaves at eight ten—[*Crosses to phone R. and sits in chair R.*]

MISS MENKEN. And you've logged a hundred thousand miles, I'll bet, just on long weekends.

LARRY. [*Puts down phone.*] Look, I don't carry a club. Just a simple no'll stop me anywhere along the line. I've got one motto—let's have fun and nobody gets hurt.

MISS MENKEN. Beautiful. Do you have it embroidered on your pajama pockets?

LARRY. Why should we kid each other? I've spent some of the best years of my life in bed. [*Small significant pause.*] What's the competition—an art gallery?

MISS MENKEN. [*Takes a deep breath, speaks as if all her resolve is melting.*] Mr. Kogen, you're right: As you suspect, I look forward with no pleasure to another weekend alone in New York. I'm hungry for the touch and the company of a man—

LARRY. [*Quietly, confident that he's just made another conquest.*] I know—

MISS MENKEN. [*Evenly, looking him straight in the eye.*] But no sonofabitch like you is going to push me over! Thanks for the coffee.

[*She turns to go out of the showroom.* LARRY *steps in front of her; she whirls away from him and goes into Morris' office and closes the door, standing with her back against it.* LARRY *goes to the door, tries to open it.*]

LARRY. Laura—

MORRIS. [*He enters L. 1, takes in the scene.*] Larry— [*He goes toward him.*] What's going on? [LARRY, *uncertain for a moment, glares at* MORRIS, *gestures helpless disturbance and anger, and strides past* MORRIS *out of the showroom and off L. 2.* MORRIS *looks after him for a moment, then goes into his office. By this time,* MISS MENKEN *is seated at his desk, with a hand over her face. She looks up as* MORRIS *enters.*] Miss Menken —what is it—?

MISS MENKEN. Oh—I was hoping I could see you. [*Distractedly, to cover her emotion.*] I thought I'd show you Number six-thirty-eight.

MORRIS. Miss Menken—never mind six-thirty-eight—what was this just now with you and Larry?

MISS MENKEN. [*After a beat.*] He's made me an offer.

MORRIS. Why should you be an exception? [*As she looks away.*] I saw you with him at Manny's. First, it's the coffee—then, I suppose, he painted you a beautiful picture of a weekend in Miami Beach—

MISS MENKEN. Yes—in broad strokes, with his usual colorful style—

MORRIS. [*Turning away.*] Well—you got nice weather for it.

MISS MENKEN. [*She looks at him, her face flushing.*] I'd better get back to my office. Excuse me. [*She starts to exit to showroom, then turns back.*]

MISS MENKEN & MORRIS. [*Together.*] I'm sorry.

MISS MENKEN. I shouldn't have stalked out like that—

MORRIS. No, I shouldn't have said what I did. [*A beat.*] I got no right to tell you what to do or not to do. You're a grown woman.

MISS MENKEN. Yes—over twenty-one. I've just heard that. "Let's have fun and nobody gets hurt." Famous last words.

MORRIS. So what's your problem? Nobody's forcing you.

MISS MENKEN. Mr. Seidman, do you have any idea what a moonscape this city turns into on a Sunday morning when you're living alone?

MORRIS. Could I ask you a personal question? *Why* are you alone? Somebody like you—beautiful, talented— [*Wryly.*]—overpaid—

MISS MENKEN. [*Smiles.*] Don't think it isn't one of the difficulties, making more than most men do.

MORRIS. Look, we can reduce it.

MISS MENKEN. No, thanks. But seriously—if you ask me do I like my way of life, yes and no. I mean, some of it I like very much. The privacy, the convenience. I just go around hoping I'll meet *some* man who makes all that seem irrelevant. Am I making any sense?

MORRIS. I understand you, Miss Menken. I mean—I understand what you are saying.

MISS MENKEN. [*Turning away.*] You know, I suddenly feel rather foolish, running on about my troubles when you have so many more important ones to deal with.

MORRIS. Well, to tell the the truth—I had a full day— a very full day.

MISS MENKEN. Would it help to talk about it?

MORRIS. [*With a sigh, crosses up to desk.*] I don't know. I had a thing with my son. [*Then.*] This much I know. I don't want to go home now. My wife will know right away something is wrong. It's like some kind of radar between us. It's enough *I'm* upset. [*A sudden idea.*] Miss Menken, how would you like to go with me for dinner—maybe afterwards to a movie—

MISS MENKEN. Oh, I'd like that very much. Matter of fact, there's an Italian movie in my neighborhood I've been wanting to see. "Traviata."

MORRIS. The opera?

MISS MENKEN. Yes. La Scala. With Cerquetti. I heard her in Rome. She's marvelous.

MORRIS. [*Crossing to his office.*] Fine. It's my favorite opera. [*Flips the* INTERCOM *switch.*]

MISS MENKEN. I'll get my coat. [*She goes out into showroom.*]

MORRIS. [*To* INTERCOM.] Miss Weintraub, call my house and say I wouldn't be home till later.

MISS WEINTRAUB'S VOICE. What time, Mr. Seidman?

MORRIS. I don't know what time. Later. [*He gets his hat and joins* MISS MENKEN *who has been putting on her coat in showroom.*] We could go to Manny's— [*Catches himself.*] No—we better not. They got a little bird there that's not on the menu.

MISS MENKEN. Well, look, I have to change anyway. Why don't we go over to my place—?

MORRIS. Good. I'll get to meet your cat, finally.

MISS MENKEN. [*Laughing.*] I'll fix us some sandwiches or something—and we can make the early show.

MORRIS. You're sure it's not too much bother?

MISS MENKEN. No bother at all. I love being domestic.

[*They start out. The* BUZZER *sounds.* MORRIS *returns and flips the switch.*]

MISS WEINTRAUB'S VOICE. Mr. Seidman, there's a call for you.

MORRIS. Who is it?

MISS WEINTRAUB'S VOICE. Your sister. From Flushing.

MORRIS. [*With a look at* MISS MENKEN.] What, already?

[*They exit L. 1 laughing.*]

CURTAIN

ACT THREE

Scene I

SCENE: *Part of the living room of* MISS MEN-KEN'S *apartment; evening, same day. The apartment is rather elegant, as comports with* MISS MENKEN'S *taste and income.*

AT RISE: MORRIS *is seated R. at a small table opposite* MISS MENKEN, *who is seated on some cushions on the floor.* BOTH *are holding glasses of wine, and the remains of dinner are on the table. There is wine in a bucket on the table; an espresso coffee pot is on a bureau Upstage.* MISS MENKEN *is dressed very attractively. These two people are being drawn to each other, and the sense of that underlies everything they say.*

MORRIS. Delicious.

MISS MENKEN. Is it chilled enough?

MORRIS. For my taste, perfect. In my circle, you're a connoisseur if you squeeze in a little seltzer with some Manischewitz. [MISS MENKEN *laughs.* MORRIS *sighs, holds his glass up to the light.*] Beautiful color. Like the sun got caught in it.

MISS MENKEN. [*Appreciatively.*] Yes. [*She looks at him, warming herself at this moment of mutual under-*

standing. After a beat, he looks over—finds her eyes on him. Rising quickly.] I'll see about the coffee. [*She goes U.R. to bureau, fills two cups with espresso.*]

MORRIS. You spent a lot of time there in Italy?

MISS MENKEN. Over two years.

MORRIS. It was on account of somebody? A young man?

MISS MENKEN. Yes. Very young. We both were, I guess. [*Returns with a cup of espresso which she places before* MORRIS.]

MORRIS. Espresso, you call this?

MISS MENKEN. Um-hm. It's served with steamed milk sometimes. They call it cappuccino. [*She gets a cup of espresso for herself, walks to C. above table.*]

MORRIS. Cappuccino. That language. Like music. [*Remembering, from far back.*] *Di quell' amor, quell' amor, che palpito dell' universo.*

MISS MENKEN. That's lovely. What is it from?

MORRIS. I don't know. I remember it from a fruit peddler in our old neighborhood.

MISS MENKEN. [*Animatedly, sitting again L. of table.*] You know what was the most wonderful thing for me of all that time in Italy? The talk. People really talk there. With their eyes, their gestures, their hearts. It spoiled me. Men don't talk to you here. They talk at you, or around you. They promote or argue or wisecrack. You'd love Italy. You'd be right at home there.

MORRIS. Laura, maybe you mean I've been talking too much?

MISS MENKEN. What I'm trying to tell you is that for the first time in a long while—a very long while—I have the feeling that conversation was made for people to discover each other, not to hide from one another.

MORRIS. I guess this is why I could talk to you. [*A remembrance crosses his mind.*] Years ago, when I was in night school, I wrote an essay. The first time entirely in English. I put a title on it, kind of fancy: "An Immigrant Looks At America." Well, you could imagine—literature it wasn't. But the teacher read it to the class and she told me afterwards I had the soul of an artist. Made a big impression on my mind.

MISS MENKEN. She was right. [*The* PHONE *rings. They turn to look at the phone.* BOTH *suspect who may be calling.* MISS MENKEN *would like to ignore it but the phone keeps ringing.*] Excuse me. [*She goes to phone on small table. L.*] Hello . . . I'm perfectly fine, thank you . . . No, I'm busy . . . No, I'm sorry, I'll be busy tomorrow, too . . . There isn't anything to discuss . . . No, please don't, I won't be here . . . I'm sorry. Goodbye

MORRIS. Larry?

MISS MENKEN. He's very confused, poor man. I don't fit into his little black book and he just can't understand it. [*Crosses Upstage to window from which the lights of the city can be seen.*]

MORRIS. What did he say?

MISS MENKEN. What am I doing to fill up my day tomorrow. Terribly concerned about me—all at once.

[*A slight pause.*]

MORRIS. So? What *are* you doing tomorrow?

MISS MENKEN. [*Coming slowly down to table.*] Well, I'll sleep late—then bathe, have a leisurely breakfast. Then, maybe—there's a showing of Dubuffet I've been wanting to see—

MORRIS. I could come with you, if you want.

MISS MENKEN. [*Smiles.*] You still feel you have to bolster my morale?

MORRIS. How do you know it's not my morale needs bolstering? [MISS MENKEN *turns abruptly and crosses to where her bag is lying on telephone table. She takes out a handkerchief, sits on sofa L. and dabs her eyes.* MORRIS *rises and crosses to her.*] Laura—darling—

MISS MENKEN. Don't mind me. I'm just exercising my female prerogative. I do it about twice a year—once with the spring line and once with the fall.

[*Her back is turned and* MORRIS *restrains an impulse to touch her.*]

MORRIS. You're all right?

MISS MENKEN. Fine now. [*Turns to him with a smile.*] I've learned to deal with almost everything on equal terms with men. Except tenderness. That still throws me.

MORRIS. [*Earnestly.*] You got to look on both sides of the ledger. So, on the debit side, you made a couple mistakes in your life—

MISS MENKEN. [*Ironically.*] Well, at least I can't make too many more. I'm thirty-three years old.

MORRIS. Thirty-three. So what should *I* say? [*Sits on sofa with her.*] Look on the credit side. You're a lovely woman—talented—

MISS MENKEN. [*Resting her head on his shoulder with a weary sigh.*] Yes—Laura Menken, winner of the Oscar for cockeyed design.

MORRIS. [*Putting his arms around her, comfortingly.*] Don't talk foolishness.

MISS MENKEN. I'm tired of the battle, Morris. I'm tired of all the propositions I've had. I'm tired of preparing a face to "meet the faces that I meet"—I'm tired of deciding—not deciding—

MORRIS. Shsh. [*He holds her tightly and she returns the intensity of the embrace. The kiss is very near—and all that it might entail for them is also very near—and perilous. After a long moment MORRIS' arms weaken their hold on her, his hands move to her shoulders and very gently he draws back.*] It's getting late. We still have time to catch the last show.

MISS MENKEN. [*After a long moment.*] Let's skip the movie. It'll get you home too late.

MORRIS. "Traviata." [*Rising, he crosses R.C., he fumbles for something to say, doesn't find it. He walks to the window.*] You know the first time I ever saw "Traviata"? It was with my wife. She wasn't my wife yet. She was a very beautiful girl, Miss Sophie Frisch. I met her at a cousin's house in Newark. It was fixed up I should drop in for a glass of tea. That's how it was done in those days. Dropped in—you could imagine. Newark. From Delancey Street. Afterwards she sent me a book, "Les Miserables" by Victor Hugo. And I sent her a book of poetry, Byron's. And the next time I saw her, we went to the opera. "Traviata." And then we were engaged. [*He turns to face her now and their eyes meet. Perhaps hers are a little misty.*] Laura, I'm not a romantic man. I'm a business man. I made from my life what I could. But, believe me, I still got a real appreciation of what a lovely young woman like you could mean to a man. But what could it be? A package of remnants I would bring you Wednesday afternoons and maybe Saturday? It's not for you, Laura, it's not for me.

MISS MENKEN. Morris, the wonderful thing about a man like you is that whatever you'd give could never be remnants. [*Rises and crosses to him.*] I wonder if you realize what a precious thing you've given me this evening. The chance to value myself as a woman again. A rich woman, with gifts to give. Like a glass of wine with the sun caught in it. You've said I was lovely. You've made me feel it. I'll always remember you for that.

MORRIS. Laura—these couple hours here tonight, I wouldn't give them away for anything in the world. I'll never forget them. [*He turns and their eyes meet. After a beat, she turns and reaches for a cigarette which she proceeds to light.* CHIMES *sound.* MISS MENKEN *wheels toward the door. The* SOUND *is repeated.*] Better answer. Maybe it's a telegram or something. [*She crushes out her cigarette, then crosses and opens the door Offstage.*]

LARRY. [*Offstage, defensively.*] Now, wait a minute. don't slug me. I just wanted to—

MISS MENKEN. [*Offstage.*] What do you mean, barging in here—?

LARRY. [*Offstage.*] It wasn't easy, if you want to know. [*He enters, holding a wrapped bottle of champagne.* MISS MENKEN *follows.*] I called you from a booth on the corner and—[*Sees* MORRIS *and is taken aback.*] Morris—

MORRIS. Hello, Larry. You're back from Miami?

LARRY. I'm sorry, Laura. You didn't say you had—company.

MISS MENKEN. I don't have to say anything to you about anything.

LARRY. No, you don't. [*He becomes aware of his surroundings. The taste and elegance of the room strikes at his feeling of inferiority, but he tries to hide it—not too successfully.*] Quite a place you got here. [*Seeing the wine and other things on the table.*] Cosy, too. [*To* MORRIS.] You're doing all right, Morris. Espresso, vintage wines—

MISS MENKEN. If you've finished your tour of inspection, Mr. Kogen—

LARRY. Yeah—I'm finished. [*He starts to the door, then stops and turns to* MORRIS.] I'm going home now, Morris. Why don't you do the same?

MORRIS. What is it, Larry? For me only vanilla?

LARRY. What about that beautiful piece of velvet you made me a speech about? [*As* MORRIS *looks at him with concealed approval.*] Go home, Morris, you've got what the rest of us are still looking for.

MISS MENKEN. Mr. Kogen, you came in on a note of apology. Do you insist on leaving the same way? If you want to know, we were just going to a movie.

[LARRY *looks from one to the other, and his last remaining vestige of self-esteem shreds away.*]

LARRY. [*Crosses to her.*] I'm sorry, Laura. [*Shakes his head, wry grin.*] This is my big day for apologies. [*Holds out bottle.*] Here, you may as well take this. It was supposed to be a little peace offering for that crummy pitch I handed you this afternoon. You'll never believe this, but it didn't start out to *be* a proposition. Ever since I came back from the road I've been trying to tell you something. That I'm sick of stuffing myself with penny candy. [*Puts bottle down.*] Well—I'll just leave this here. It's champagne, by the way. With my luck, it's probably the wrong year. [*He turns, and strides out L.*]

[MISS MENKEN *takes a few steps toward the door, looking after him.* MORRIS *watches her closely.*]

MORRIS. You didn't think he could be hurt, did you?

MISS MENKEN. No—

MORRIS. Neither did I.

MISS MENKEN. [*Distractedly.*] Why do I feel so awful? I—I didn't want to hurt him, really.

MORRIS. Who knows? Have you been blaming him maybe for the others? [*She looks at him. After a pause.*] Well, you had enough for one night. Get some rest. [*He goes to table behind sofa and gets his coat and hat. Humorously.*] I agree with you about the movie. We both cried enough over "Traviata." All that singing and suffering—who needs it? [*Tenderly.*] Good night—Miss Menken.

MISS MENKEN. Good night—Mr. Seidman.

[*She extends her hand for a handshake. He holds her hand for a moment of complete understanding—then exits. Her eyes go to the champagne bottle* LARRY *has left.*]

FADE OUT

ACT THREE

Scene II

SCENE: *The Seidman bedroom. Immediately following.*

AT RISE: SOPHIE *is at her dressing table, in an elaborate new nightgown, her hair carefully done up—without the "hardware store."* MORRIS *enters from D.L. to L. of bed.*

MORRIS. You're up?

SOPHIE. I'm up.

[*There's a moment as she waits for him to notice her appearance.*]

MORRIS. So—what's new?

[*She gives him a reproachful look as he starts taking off his jacket.*]

SOPHIE. You were in the shop all this time?

MORRIS. Yes. I had something to attend to.

SOPHIE. Did you have your phone disconnected? I tried to call you half a dozen times.

MORRIS. [*Defensively.*] What was so important? [*He hangs up his coat.*]

SOPHIE. What was so important in the *shop* tonight, Morris?

MORRIS. You want an answer? Or your FBI already gave you a report?

SOPHIE. I don't need a report. You've got lipstick all over you.

MORRIS. [*Picks up a hand mirror and looks into it.*] It's not all over. It's just on my collar. A little.

SOPHIE. Your precious designer, I suppose, with her problems. And your son with his girl friend. Two of a kind.

MORRIS. What you got against me I understand, Sophie. [*Sits in chair L.*] I've been a playboy all my life. But Harold—

SOPHIE. All this talk about independence, having to be on his own—it's that girl, that's all. Pure and simple.

MORRIS. Well, for a girl, pure and simple is a very nice recommendation.

[*She flashes him a bitter look.*]

HAROLD'S VOICE. [*Offstage.*] Pa—

MORRIS. [*Turning.*] Yes—?

HAROLD'S VOICE. Are you decent?

SOPHIE. [*Sotto voce.*] That's a good question.

MORRIS. [*Flashing his* WIFE *a baleful glance.*] Come in, Harold.

[HAROLD *enters from D.R. to R. of bed. He and his* FATHER *look at each other in a moment of constraint.* HAROLD *is obviously feeling contrite, as is* MORRIS. HAROLD *carries a suitcase which he sets down at R.*]

HAROLD. [*Diffidently.*] Is it all right for me to use one of your suitcases, Pa? Mine are all too small.

MORRIS. What do you need suitcases?

SOPHIE. He's moving out. Didn't he tell you?

MORRIS. [*After a moment.*] No. You're mad at me, Harold?

HAROLD. [*Crossing to* MORRIS.] That's got nothing to do with it, Pa. All that stuff I let loose at you this afternoon—I should have got my head knocked off.

MORRIS. When are you going?

HAROLD. I thought in the morning. I got a nice place, Pa. No cockroaches. And I can use my typewriter all night.

SOPHIE. [*Rises, goes to bed.*] You're not planning to sleep at all in this new, independent life of yours? Oh, yes, I forgot—the important thing in life is being awake.

[*Sits at R. side of bed.*]

HAROLD. [*Gently.*] I'll sleep, Ma.

SOPHIE. So this is what came of all our plans for you, Harold?

HAROLD. [*Sits at L. side of bed.*] Ma, it's my life. Supposed to be. I have plans of my own—first of all to find out what I really want to do. And I've got to be on my own for that. [*Almost despairingly.*] If only I could make you understand somehow.

SOPHIE. I understand, Harold. I don't *want* to—but I'm afraid I understand. [*She strokes his hair for a few moments. Then suddenly, she remembers something.*]

Oh, I forgot—I took in your brown cordovan shoes for soles and heels. They'll be ready in the morning.

HAROLD. Thanks. [*There's a moment. Then he turns to his* FATHER.] Pa, I wanted to thank you, what you did for the Sowolskas.

MORRIS. Well, I don't like it—this business of dispossess, furniture on the street. Brings back too many memories.

HAROLD. Kind of lousy what goes on in the world, isn't it?

MORRIS. The world is a world. Maybe if people would be people, would be a better world. [*Looking at* HAROLD.] And I want to take back what I said to you. Maybe it's *only* for amateurs who are not afraid to mix in, to get a bloody nose. Older people, we want to wait, think things over. Young people, with a heart and a conscience, they want the world to be a better place, not next century, not next year, but tomorrow morning. Maybe this is the best hope for the world.

HAROLD. [*After a pause.*] You look tired, Pa.

MORRIS. I'll be all right. A night's sleep.

[HAROLD *rises from bed and crosses to door R. Many thoughts crowd his mind—but above all the thought that his debt to his father demands something of him. Impulsively, he sets down the suitcase, and turns.*]

HAROLD. Pa, look— You're part of my world too—you and Ma. I know I've messed things up—but if you really want me in the shop—You said yesterday you thought I could learn. Well, I'm willing to give it another try. I'll pipe down, I promise. No more lectures to Karp—no more—

MORRIS. No, Harold. I don't want you in the shop. You're fired. [*Rises, crosses to* HAROLD.] I wasn't honest with you. I thought—well, in the shop at least I would have you near me, you'd learn the value of a dollar, you'd buckle down gradually— [*With a gesture of dismissal.*] I don't want it now. Go, do what you want to do. Be what you want to be. A writer, or a poet or a clamshell—whatever it is. Give yourself a chance. Because if you wouldn't, will come a day when it will be like a fist in your stomach and whatever else you got wouldn't mean a thing. Go. Have your own struggle and your own dreams. Make your own mistakes. You're entitled. [*He gives the boy a wry smile. They squeeze each other's arms—the closest they can come to a full embrace.*]

HAROLD. Thanks, Pa. I—I'll keep in touch— [HAROLD *takes in both his* FATHER *and* MOTHER *for a moment— then he turns abruptly, picks up his suitcase, and hurries out R.*]

MORRIS. [*After a pause.*] Well, about this boy we don't have to worry. Whatever he'll do, wherever he'll go, he'll be a mench.

SOPHIE. And when will you start being a mench? [*She starts to cry.*]

MORRIS. Ah-ha—the faucet.

SOPHIE. After twenty-five years of living together there ought to be some communication between people. Run to somebody else to tell her stories about your miserable

home life—and get yourself smeared with her lipstick—
a man your age—

MORRIS. What do you mean, a man my age? You think
I dropped dead in this department? Let me tell you a
secret, Sophie. A man who is faithful to his wife
twenty-five years, it's not because he didn't have maybe
other ideas sometimes. It's because he made a decision
how he wants to live. What do you think, I'm a statue?
I'm immune? What do you know about me, Sophie?
Your husband? You know I go down to the office every
day, I come home every night, I holler, I make jokes.
Suppose I would tell you I got feelings, sometimes, got
nothing to do with my business, my obligations—like
I would want to swallow the whole world and still it
wouldn't be enough? That sometimes I would like to
be a bird and fly away from all the responsibilities,
home, family, everything. Suppose I would tell you that
sometimes when I'm working late in the shop, I put
away the patterns and I'm thinking—what is it for?
Where is my life? Where did it go? What did it count
for? Thirty years—worry, aggravation, fights. A rating
in Dun and Bradstreet? A room full of piece goods?
Boxes of buttons? Is this something to show for a life-
time?

SOPHIE. I thought maybe a man would figure his family,
his home, his wife. Twenty-five years of love—loyalty—

MORRIS. Loyalty is a beautiful thing, Sophie. [*Rises
and moves to L. of* SOPHIE.] But there's other things
in life got nothing to do with loyalty. I'll make you a
confession. I lied to you tonight about having something
to do in the shop. I didn't want to come home tonight.
I wanted to spend an evening with another woman. Take

her to an Italian movie. [*He comes close to her.*] After all these years, I have to tell you this? I love you, Sophie. You're my whole life. Without you I got nothing. But tonight I turned to another woman. For a minute I was her hero, not because I'm young and handsome—but because I gave her a little understanding, a little tenderness. And for me, too, she was—[*Sits on the bed.*] do I know her name? Helen of Troy? Venus? Miss America? Miss Menken? [*Pauses, defeated by his inability to express the inexpressible.*] All right, Sophie. I told you the truth. You want a divorce?

SOPHIE. Your Helen of Troy—did she give you something to eat at least?

MORRIS. [*Brightening happily.*] Sophie—[*They embrace.*] I'll tell you a joke, Sophie. I didn't even kiss her. The lipstick on my collar—she put her head on my shoulder. You know why? Because she was grateful. I reminded her for a minute of a young man in Italy she was in love with long ago—who talked a lot.

SOPHIE. As long as you talked a lot.

MORRIS. Sophie! You know what? We're going to take a trip—to Italy.

SOPHIE. Italy? Why Italy all of a sudden?

MORRIS. Ah, you don't know, Sophie. The ruins alone— the music—the people—the way they talk, from the heart—

SOPHIE. How would we know if it's in Italian?

MORRIS. Look, don't always throw a damper, I mean it, Sophie. We're young yet, we got a million things to enjoy.

SOPHIE. Morris—

MORRIS. Now, don't give me any arguments. I made up my mind and you know that when I decide it's no use talking. This is the way it's going to be. What is it—I have to be swallowed alive by my business? We're going to Italy!

SOPHIE. All right, Morris. When?

MORRIS. When? When the line is finished! [*He catches the look on her face. They both laugh and go to each other.*] Sophie!

CURTAIN